K-1 INSTANT Math Centers

HANDS-ON INDEPENDENT MATH ACTIVITIES

CONTRIBUTING WRITERS
Karen Bauer, Janet Bruno, Rosa Drew, Caroline Ellis,
Mary Kurth, Sue Lewis, and Cathy Young

EDITOR
Ruth Simon

ILLUSTRATOR
Kathleen Dunne

COVER ILLUSTRATOR
Eddie Young

DESIGNER
Marek/Janci Design

COVER DESIGNER
Moonhee Pak

ART DIRECTOR
Tom Cochrane

PROJECT DIRECTOR
Carolea Williams

Table of Contents

Introduction

Instant Math Centers is designed to offer a great supplement to your primary math program, providing reinforcement of basic math skills through practical, hands-on application in a format students will enjoy.

Instant Math Centers consists of 51 center activities within 15 math skill areas. Each skill section begins with a one-page overview of the center activities in that math skill area, including materials needed and teaching tips and extensions. The ☆ icon indicates teacher preparation that is required for an activity. The bulleted items are optional teaching tips and extensions. Each center activity includes a task card and accompanying activity sheets—all reproducible for instant student use.

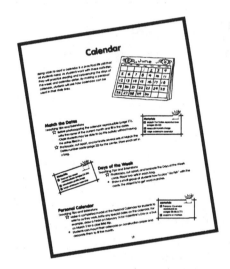

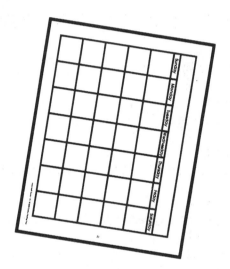

Each task card presents step-by-step directions, simply written and clearly illustrated, plus a Challenge or Math Journal activity. The illustrations show students exactly what to do, making the activities easy to follow, even for beginning readers and those with limited English language skills.

Instant Math Centers is designed to help students build a strong mathematical foundation and gives them experiences in all content and process areas of the National Council of Teachers of Mathematics standards as follows:

- number and operation
- patterns, functions, and algebra
- geometry and spatial sense
- measurement
- data analysis, statistics, and probability

- problem solving
- reasoning and proof
- communication
- connections
- representations

3

How Do I Begin?

Create a Math Center

A classroom math center should include a variety of materials for students to manipulate and enough space in which to work. There should be opportunities for free exploration and discovery, as well as specifically directed activities, which is where *Instant Math Centers* offers the perfect solution.

The physical setup could be as limited, small, and isolated as a desk with a study carrel around it, one or more math center activities, and the materials for those activities.

If space allows, you can use an entire corner of the classroom for your math center. A center with tables, countertop space, and a carpeted area allows students to work on a variety of activities. Store activity materials on shelves and in drawers and containers for easy access by students.

Gather Materials

The initial preparation is simply to reproduce the pages needed for the activities you have chosen. Feel free to enhance the task cards and activity sheets by coloring them. For durability and long-term use, mount them on tagboard, and then laminate them or store them in plastic or acetate pocket sheet protectors.

In addition to a generous supply of paper and pencils, the materials needed to implement *Instant Math Centers* in your classroom are a combination of common household items and commercial math manipulatives, such as linking cubes and pattern blocks. The easiest way to begin is to send home a letter with a list of requested items at the beginning of the year. Use the reproducible letter to parents on page 5, or create one of your own. Prepare a sorting area, and have students help you organize the materials.

Dear Parents,

We are asking for your help in collecting materials to use in our math program. We will use these materials for adding, subtracting, sorting, measuring, estimating, and counting. Please don't purchase items especially for us. Just see if you have any of these items at home that you may no longer need. If you can, please send any of the items listed below.

- buttons, beads, spools, clothespins, marbles, shells, yarn, string, shoelaces, socks

- small rocks, stones, pinecones, nuts, bolts, screws, washers, old keys, bottle caps, small lids, poker chips, dice

- pasta (macaroni in assorted colors and shapes, shells, spirals, etc.), dry beans in assorted colors (pinto, navy, black, red, lima, etc.), popcorn (unpopped), seeds, rice, mixed nuts (shelled and unshelled), trail mix, snack mix

- measuring cups, measuring spoons, scoops, funnels, straws, coffee stirrers, craft sticks, toothpicks (flat)

- various coins, play money

- plastic containers—cups, bowls, and empty margarine tubs, food containers with lids, and film canisters

- small plastic or cardboard boxes (shoe-box size or smaller) for storing items

- paper cups, paper plates, paper bags (lunch size), resealable plastic bags

Thank you for your help.

Sincerely,

Instant! Math Centers • K–1 © 2000 Creative Teaching Press

   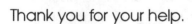

5

Introduction

How Do I Implement the Center Activities?

The simplest way to introduce your students to the activities in *Instant Math Centers* is in small groups on a rotating basis. Select activities that are appropriate for the skill level of each group. During these initial experiences, set guidelines for how to use the center, how to care for materials, and where to put finished products. Once students are familiar with the procedures, experiment with teacher-directed and self-directed options, student groupings, the number of activities, and time and space allowances.

How many students work in the math center at a time depends largely on the amount of space and materials in the center. You can limit the number of students by the number of chairs available, or make a designated number of math center necklaces or color-coded clothespins available for them to wear during their time in the math center. Students can work individually, in pairs (with a classmate or a cross-age tutor), or in small groups. You will be able to observe each student's degree of independent functioning and use this data to determine future groupings. Students who excel in a particular activity may be paired with those being introduced to that activity for the first time or with those who may need additional direction for completing the task. If space and supplies are ample and students are productively engaged, everyone wins.

The number of center activities available to the students can vary from one to many, at any given time, depending on the degree of simultaneous activity that you are comfortable with. Regardless of how many center activities are available to students, they should all be meaningful and appropriate and should reinforce or provide practice in skill areas that have already been presented.

The length of time you allot for math center activities may vary, depending on the students and the tasks. You can learn a lot about your students and their learning styles, their degree of responsibility, and their thought processes by allowing them some freedom to choose activities and then observing them as they work.

The purpose for having centers in the classroom is to provide a meaningful setting in which students can apply skills that they have already been taught. While students are thus engaged, the teacher is free to work with small groups of students, as well as circulate throughout the classroom to observe, record anecdotal notes, and offer direction as needed.

Ideally, students will have the freedom to explore a variety of hands-on activities and make choices about which activities they pursue. Making choices is as important a skill as any math skill. It is an essential part of learning to think and take responsibility for oneself.

7

How Do I Keep Track?

Many effective means of assessment are available to you. How you choose to keep track will depend on what information you value as most important to record. The reproducible activity sheets in *Instant Math Centers* can be stored in individual student folders or in a central location in the math center. These pages provide a built-in record of students' accomplishments and levels of understanding.

Teacher observation and anecdotal records can serve as invaluable tools with which to assess the needs of students, as well as a means to gain insights into their unique learning styles and thought processes. Note what choices students make. Some students may systematically go through the center activities sequentially. Some may select activities at random. Others may choose the same activity over and over again. As students are engaged in a center activity, encourage them to verbalize their findings by asking them appropriate questions about how they arrived at their conclusions.

Use the Student Checklist on page 9 to keep track of completed activities. It may be used to simply indicate which math center activities each student chooses and how often. You can also use a coding system, such as −, ?, +, or 0, /, X, to denote level of mastery, or devise your own system.

Student Checklist

Instant Math Centers • K–1 © 2000 Creative Teaching Press

Addition

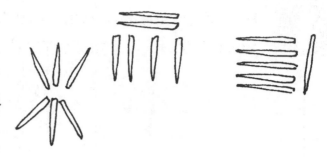

...heir addition skills as they make
...eal objects in these center activities.
...y verbalize their actions and demonstrate an
understanding of addition, they can begin using
pictures and number sentences to record their findings.

Cloud Addition
Teaching Tips and Extensions
- Laminate copies of the Cloud Addition Work Mat.
- Introduce the activity by reading aloud *It Looked Like Spilt Milk* by Charles Shaw.
- Recite cloud story problems into a tape recorder. Have students join a set of cotton-ball "clouds" for each problem.

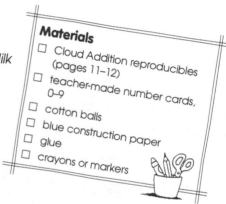

Materials
- ☐ Cloud Addition reproducibles (pages 11–12)
- ☐ teacher-made number cards, 0–9
- ☐ cotton balls
- ☐ blue construction paper
- ☐ glue
- ☐ crayons or markers

Materials
- ☐ Peanut Addition reproducibles (pages 13–14)
- ☐ several pairs of dice
- ☐ large container of peanuts in the shell

Peanut Addition
Teaching Tips and Extensions
- Laminate copies of the Peanut Addition Work Mat.
- Use simple equation cards instead of dice.

Toothpick Addition
Teaching Tips and Extensions
- Have students glue toothpicks to a piece of colored construction paper to record their favorite design.
- Have students write a number sentence to match each toothpick design.

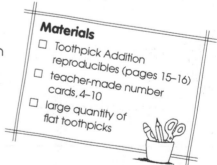

Materials
- ☐ Toothpick Addition reproducibles (pages 15–16)
- ☐ teacher-made number cards, 4–10
- ☐ large quantity of flat toothpicks

Materials
- ☐ Beans and Cups reproducibles (pages 17–18)
- ☐ teacher-made addition cards, bagged in sets of 10
- ☐ resealable plastic bags
- ☐ small paper cups
- ☐ beans
- ☐ paper for student-made addition cards

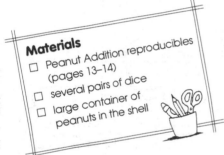

Beans and Cups
Teaching Tips and Extensions
- Change the difficulty level of the addition cards according to the needs of your students.
- For fun, spray-paint white beans a variety of colors.

Cloud Addition

1 Place 2 number cards at the top of your Cloud Addition Work Mat.

2 Count out a set of clouds (cotton balls) to match each card. Add the sets together.

3 Use different number cards to make 3 more cloud combinations.

Challenge Glue 3 cloud combinations to a piece of blue construction paper. Write an addition number sentence for each one. Draw 5 more things in your sky picture.

Addition

Cloud Addition Work Mat

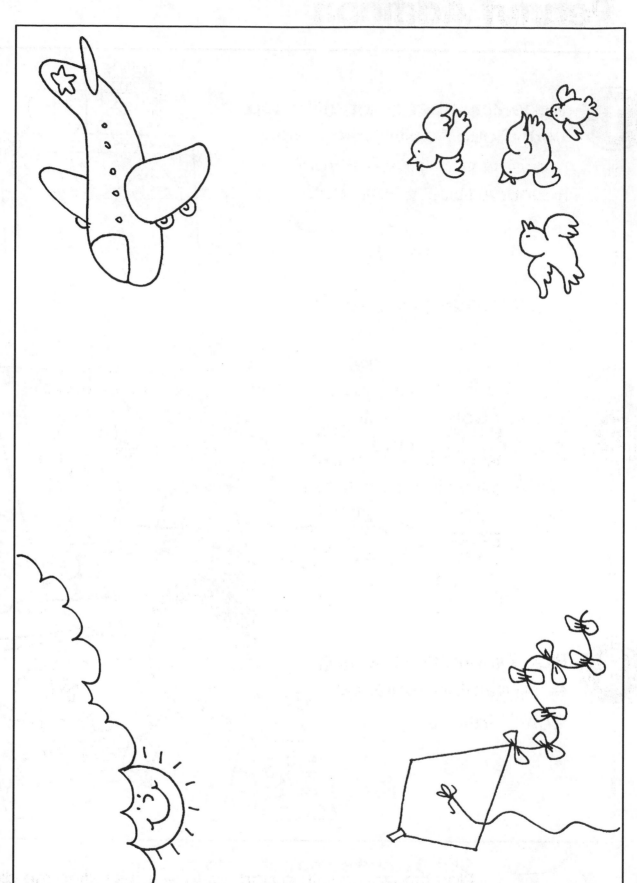

Peanut Addition

1 Roll 2 dice. Place 2 sets of peanuts that match the numbers you rolled on your Peanut Addition Work Mat.

2 Add the peanuts together. Write the addition number sentence on your work mat.

3 Play 7 more times, writing each number sentence as you go.

**Challenge** Play the game with a partner. Take turns rolling the dice to see who gets more peanuts each time you play.

Addition

Peanut Addition Work Mat

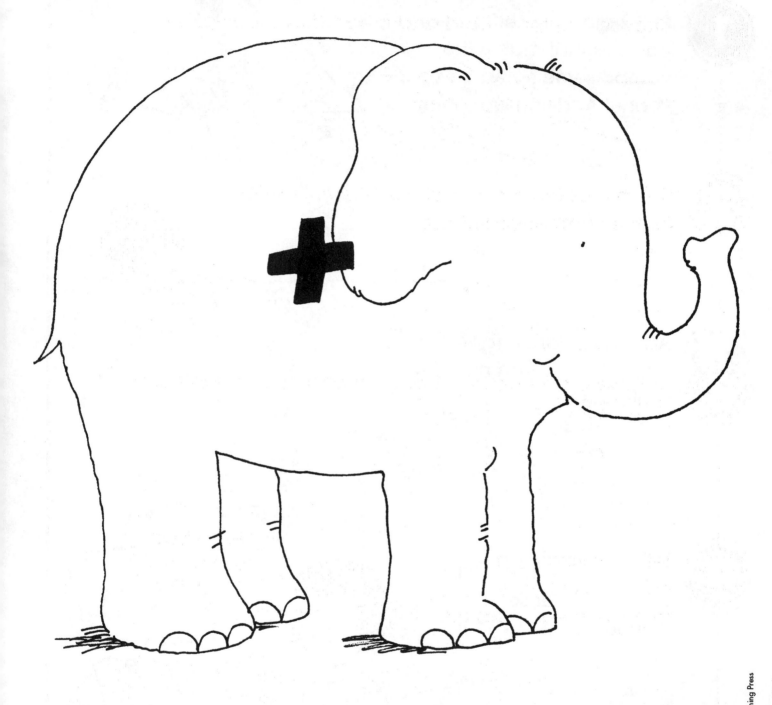

14

Toothpick Addition

1 Choose 1 number card and a handful of toothpicks.

2 Use the toothpicks to make 5 different designs for the number you chose.

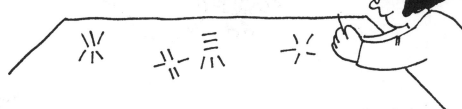

3 Choose a different number card and make 5 toothpick designs for that number.

4 Tell a classmate a number sentence to go with each design.

I have 5 up and 3 across That makes 8.

Instant Math Centers • K–1 © 2000 Creative Teaching Press

Math Journal Write about or draw your 3 favorite toothpick designs on your journal page.

Math Journal

Write about or draw your 3 favorite toothpick designs.

3+3

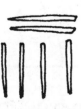

2+4

5+1

Beans and Cups

1 Empty 1 bag and lay all the addition cards faceup on the table. Place a cup near each card.

4+4

3+4

5+2

6+3

Beans

2 Put the correct number of beans in each cup as you solve each problem.

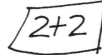

2+2

3 Write 6 of your number sentences on your Beans and Cups sheet. Draw the matching number of beans in the cups on your sheet.

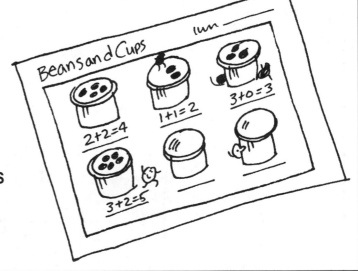

Beans and Cups

2+2=4

1+1=2

3+0=3

3+2=5

Challenge Write 3 new addition cards. Have a classmate solve each problem and count the beans into the cups.

Addition

Beans and Cups

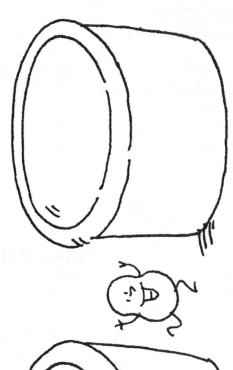

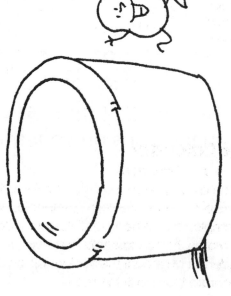

Calendar

Being able to read a calendar is a practical life skill that all students need. As students work with these activities, they will practice reading and sequencing the days of the week and calendar dates. By making a personal calendar, students will see how calendars can be used in their daily lives.

Match the Dates
Teaching Tips and Extensions

☆ Before photocopying the calendar reproducible (page 21), write the name of the current month and fill in the dates. (Older students may be able to do this activity without having the dates filled in.)

☆ Photocopy, cut apart, and laminate several sets of Match the Dates number cards (page 22) for the center. Store each set in a bag.

Materials
- ☐ Match the Dates reproducibles (pages 20–22)
- ☐ resealable plastic bags
- ☐ large classroom calendar

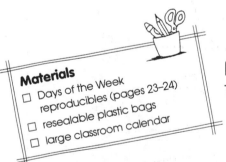

Materials
- ☐ Days of the Week reproducibles (pages 23–24)
- ☐ resealable plastic bags
- ☐ large classroom calendar

Days of the Week
Teaching Tips and Extensions

☆ Photocopy, cut apart, and laminate the Days of the Week cards. Place two sets in each bag.

● Show a small group of students how to play "Go Fish" with the cards. The object is to get word matches.

Personal Calendar
Teaching Tips and Extensions

☆ Make a completed model of the Personal Calendar for students to refer to as they work. Note any special dates on the calendar. For example, draw a heart on February 14 for Valentine's Day or a bus on March 3 for a class field trip.

● Students can mount their calendars on construction paper and decorate them to fit the month.

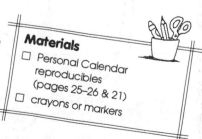

Materials
- ☐ Personal Calendar reproducibles (pages 25–26 & 21)
- ☐ crayons or markers

Match the Dates

1 Take a bag. Pull a number out of the bag. Say the number.

2 Match the number to the date on the calendar.

3 When all the dates have been matched, say them in order to a classmate. Can you read the pattern, too?

Challenge Look at your calendar with a classmate. Name a date and have him or her find that date on the calendar. What day of the week is it?

Sunday	Monday	Tuesday	Wednesday	Thursday	Friday	Saturday

Calendar

Match the Dates

△ 1	2	□ 3	△ 4	5
8	9	10	11	12
□ 15	△ 16	17	18	△ 19
△ 22	23	24	25	26
29	30	△ 31		

Days of the Week

1 Play with a partner. Empty 1 bag and spread out all the cards facedown.

2 Turn over 2 cards and read them out loud. If the cards match, keep the pair and take another turn.

Sunday! It's a match.

3 If the cards don't match, turn them back over. It's your partner's turn. Play until all the cards are matched up.

These don't match.

4 Lay out all the cards in correct order, starting with Sunday and ending with Saturday.

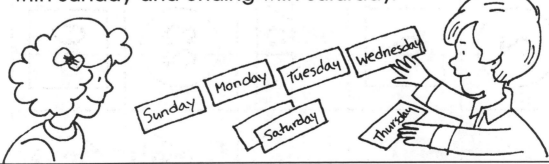

 **Challenge** Pick 1 card. Use the classroom calendar to find all the dates that come on that day of the week.

Calendar

Days of the Week

Sunday	
Monday	Tuesday
Wednesday	Thursday
Friday	Saturday

Personal Calendar

1   Write the name of the month on your calendar.

2   Fill in the dates. Be sure to start on the right day of the week.

3   Mark special days for the month.

 Write about or draw one of the special days on your journal page. Tell the date and the day of the week.

Calendar

Math Journal

Write about or draw one of the special days. Tell the date and the day of the week.

Special Day!

Instant Math Centers • K–1 © 2000 Creative Teaching Press

Counting

Students learn to count in sequential stages. The skills involved include rote counting, one-to-one correspondence, and conservation of numbers. Help students master these number concepts through the repeated, meaningful, hands-on experiences with counting real objects in these activities.

Train Cars

Teaching Tips and Extensions

- Have students work in pairs to make longer trains.
- Have students draw train cars on a long roll of paper, each student adding cars to make an even longer train.

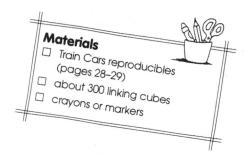

Materials
- ☐ Train Cars reproducibles (pages 28–29)
- ☐ about 300 linking cubes
- ☐ crayons or markers

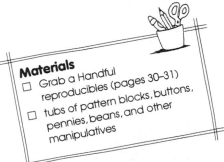

Materials
- ☐ Grab a Handful reproducibles (pages 30–31)
- ☐ tubs of pattern blocks, buttons, pennies, beans, and other manipulatives

Grab a Handful

Teaching Tips and Extensions

- Use larger-sized manipulatives for younger students so that they grab a smaller amount; use smaller manipulatives as students gain experience.
- Have students trace around their own hands on construction paper and write or draw the number of objects they can hold.

Counting Jars

Teaching Tips and Extensions

- ☆ Label jars and fill each with a set of 25–99 objects, such as rocks, shells, toothpicks, blocks, toy figures, seeds, buttons, and cubes.
- Provide small paper cups so students can group objects by tens as they count.

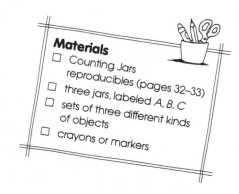

Materials
- ☐ Counting Jars reproducibles (pages 32–33)
- ☐ three jars, labeled A, B, C
- ☐ sets of three different kinds of objects
- ☐ crayons or markers

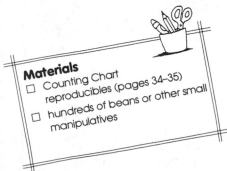

Materials
- ☐ Counting Chart reproducibles (pages 34–35)
- ☐ hundreds of beans or other small manipulatives

Counting Chart

Teaching Tips and Extensions

- Invite students to bring in collections of 100 small items to be used as counters at the center.
- Post a large hundreds chart at the center.
- Have students tape-record themselves as they count.

Train Cars

1 Connect 19 linking cubes like cars in a train. Use any color but black.

2 Make the 20th train car black.

3 Repeat the activity. Make your train longer and longer.

Math Journal Draw 20 train cars on your journal page. Draw something different in each car.

Instant Math Centers • K–1 © 2000 Creative Teaching Press

Math Journal

Draw 20 train cars. Draw something different in each car.
You can use the back of this page.

Grab a Handful

1 Play with a partner. Grab a handful of objects. Ask your partner to guess how many there are.

2 Count them together. Write the number on a Grab a Handful sheet.

3 Take turns grabbing and guessing 8 more times. Use a different object each time.

Challenge Play the same game, but grab 2 handfuls at a time.

Instant Math Centers • K–1 © 2000 Creative Teaching Press

Grab a Handful

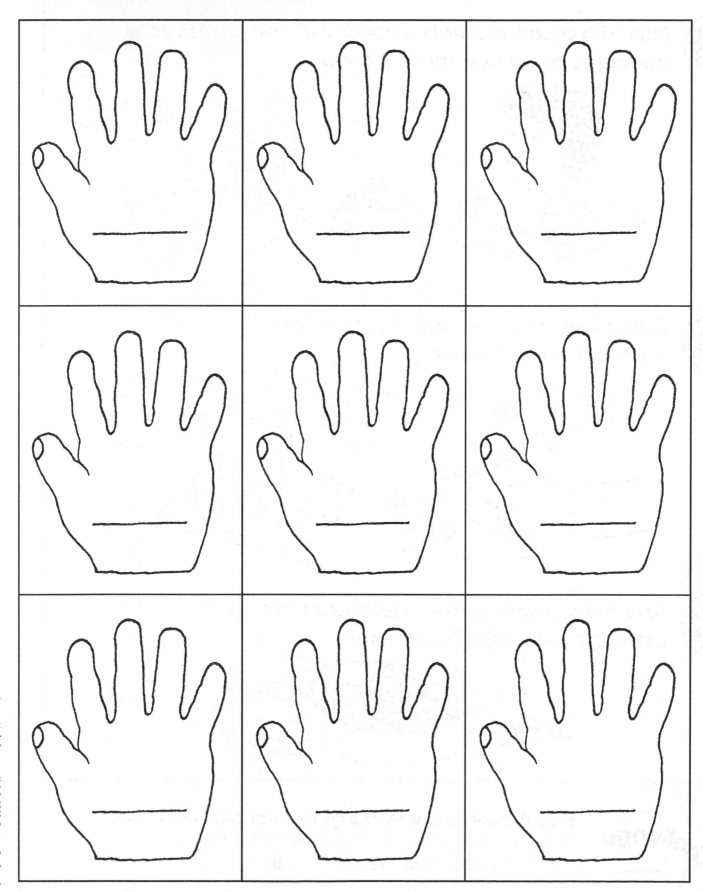

Counting

Counting Jars

1 Spill out and count the objects in 1 of the jars.

25, 26, 27...

2 Draw a picture of the objects you counted on your Counting Jars sheet. Write the number on your sheet.

3 Repeat the activity with the other 2 jars.

Challenge Take a handful of objects from each jar. Count how many objects you have all together. Then sort them back into the correct jars.

Instant Math Centers • K–1 © 2000 Creative Teaching Press

Name _____

A

B

C

Counting Chart

1 Place a bean on each number of your Counting Chart.

2 Remove the beans 1 at a time, beginning with 1 and ending with 100. Count out loud as you work.

76, 77, 78...

3 Place a bean anywhere on the chart. Have a partner "count on" from that number to 100.

47, 48, 49...

Challenge Start on 2 and place beans on every other number. Then count out loud by 2s to 100.

Counting

Counting Chart

1	2	3	4	5	6	7	8	9	10
11	12	13	14	15	16	17	18	19	20
21	22	23	24	25	26	27	28	29	30
31	32	33	34	35	36	37	38	39	40
41	42	43	44	45	46	47	48	49	50
51	52	53	54	55	56	57	58	59	60
61	62	63	64	65	66	67	68	69	70
71	72	73	74	75	76	77	78	79	80
81	82	83	84	85	86	87	88	89	90
91	92	93	94	95	96	97	98	99	100

Estimating

Each day, students are presented with many situations that require estimation (e.g., I think my sandwich will fit in this size bag, or I'll probably get three more turns before the bell rings.). Use these center activities to help students develop basic strategies for arriving at reasonable estimates and to refine their estimates.

How Many?
Teaching Tips and Extensions

- Start off with a smaller number of objects and increase the number as students' estimation skills improve.
- Make this an ongoing activity by frequently changing the objects and number of objects in the jars.

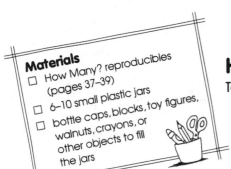

Materials
- ☐ How Many? reproducibles (pages 37–39)
- ☐ 6–10 small plastic jars
- ☐ bottle caps, blocks, toy figures, walnuts, crayons, or other objects to fill the jars

Guess How Long
Teaching Tips and Extensions

- Substitute other nonstandard units of measure (e.g., paper clips, lima beans, wooden cubes) for the linking cubes.
- Estimation Homework: How many hands tall is your mom or dad? Guess and count!

Materials
- ☐ Guess How Long reproducibles (pages 40–41)
- ☐ assortment of 6–12 objects to measure (e.g., blocks, string, pencils, spoons)
- ☐ linking cubes

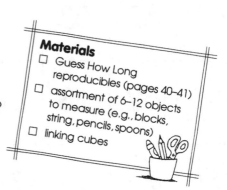

Materials
- ☐ How Many Scoops? reproducibles (pages 42 & 38)
- ☐ drop cloth
- ☐ 6–10 small plastic jars labeled with letters of the alphabet
- ☐ 6 small uniform scoops (e.g., ¹/₄ cup, tablespoon, coffee scoop)
- ☐ tubs of rice, birdseed, or small beans

How Many Scoops?
Teaching Tips and Extensions

- ☆ Cover the work area with a drop cloth.
- Show students how to fill each scoop with a full, level measure.
- Estimation Homework: How many scoops of cereal does your breakfast bowl hold?

How Many?

1 Choose 1 jar. Estimate how many objects are in the jar.

2 On your Guess and Count sheet, draw 1 of the objects in the jar and write your estimate.

3 Count the objects in the jar. Write the number on your sheet.

4 Repeat the activity with 5 more jars.

Math Journal What would you choose to fill a jar with? Draw the jar on your journal page and tell how many of your chosen objects you think could fit in it.

Name _____

Guess and Count

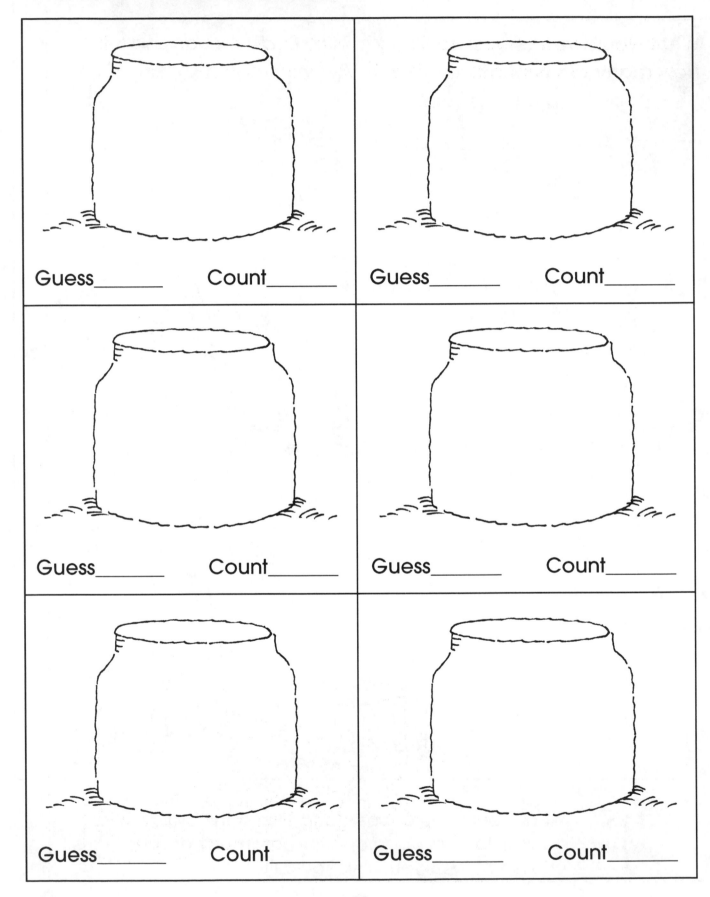

Guess_____   Count_____

Guess_____   Count_____

Guess_____   Count_____

Guess_____   Count_____

Guess_____   Count_____

Guess_____   Count_____

Math Journal

What would you choose to fill a jar with? Draw the jar and tell how many of your chosen objects you think could fit in it.

Instant Math Centers • K-1 © 2000 Creative Teaching Press

Estimating

Guess How Long

1 Choose 1 object. Guess how many linking cubes long it is.

2 Draw the object and write your guess on your Guess How Long sheet.

3 Measure the object with the cubes. Write your answer on your sheet.

4 Repeat the activity with 5 other objects.

 **Challenge** Find something in your classroom that is about 50 cubes long. Can you find something about 100 cubes long?

Instant Math Centers • K–1 © 2000 Creative Teaching Press

Name _____

Guess How Long

Guess_____   Count_____   Guess_____   Count_____

Guess_____   Count_____   Guess_____   Count_____

Guess_____   Count_____   Guess_____   Count_____

Estimating

How Many Scoops?

1 Choose 1 jar and 1 scoop. Guess how many scoops will fill the jar.

2 Write the letter of the jar and your estimate on your Guess and Count sheet.

3 Count the scoops as you fill the jar. Write the number on your sheet.

4 Repeat the activity with 5 other jars. Use different scoops.

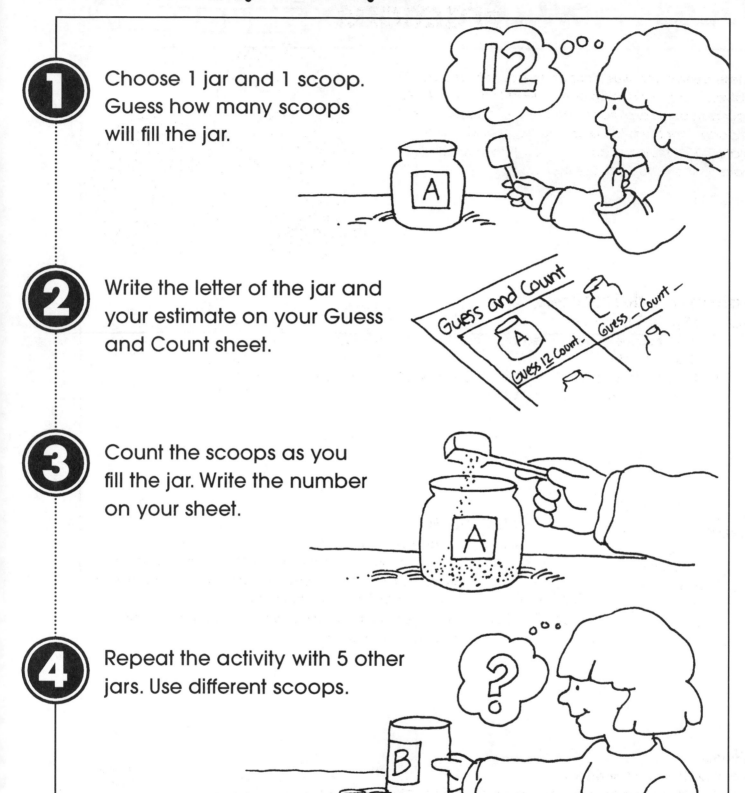

 **Challenge** Work with a partner. Arrange any 3 jars from smallest to largest. Can you arrange 5 jars from smallest to largest?

Fractions

These center activities focus on the identification of halves, fourths, and thirds as equal parts of a whole. As young students explore the concept of fractions, it is important for them to be able to handle concrete materials so they can actually match the fractional parts to see if the parts are equal in size.

Pattern Block Fractions
Teaching Tips and Extensions

- Introduce the activity by reading aloud *Eating Fractions* by Bruce McMillan.
- Invite students to trace one of their designs on a piece of paper and color in the pattern block shapes.

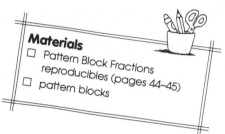

Materials
- ☐ Pattern Block Fractions reproducibles (pages 44–45)
- ☐ pattern blocks

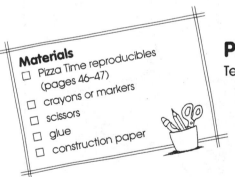

Materials
- ☐ Pizza Time reproducibles (pages 46–47)
- ☐ crayons or markers
- ☐ scissors
- ☐ glue
- ☐ construction paper

Pizza Time
Teaching Tips and Extensions

- Partners can play "Concentration" with two sets of pizza slices. All slices are placed facedown. Students turn over two slices at a time, trying to find a matching pair.
- Invite students to make pizzas from clay or play dough and cut the pizzas into equal slices.

Walls
Teaching Tips and Extensions

- Let students learn by trial and error how many blocks long to build "walls" that can be divided into equal parts.
- Use small wooden blocks instead of linking cubes.

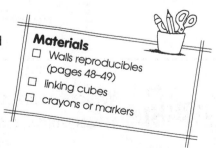

Materials
- ☐ Walls reproducibles (pages 48–49)
- ☐ linking cubes
- ☐ crayons or markers

Pattern Block Fractions

1 Use the pattern blocks to make 4 different shapes each with 2 equal parts (halves).

2 Use the pattern blocks to make 4 different shapes each with 4 equal parts (fourths).

3 Use the pattern blocks to make 4 different shapes each with 3 equal parts (thirds).

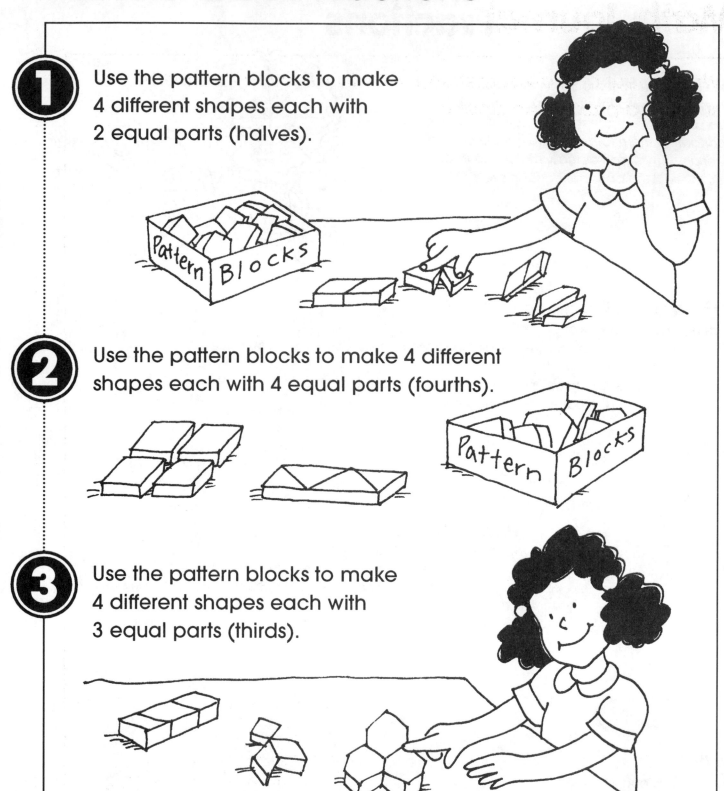

Write about or draw something you divide into equal parts, such as a pizza or an apple, on your journal page.

Name _____

Math Journal

Write about or draw something you divide into equal parts, such as a pizza or an apple.

Fractions

Pizza Time

1 Color and cut apart the 3 pizzas on your Pizza Time sheet.

2 Mix up the slices, and then put them back together to make 3 whole pizzas.

3 Glue each whole pizza on a piece of construction paper.

4 Draw faces to show how many friends could share each pizza.

Challenge Draw your own pizza on a sheet of paper. Cut it into equal portions. Write the fraction for each slice.

Pizza Time

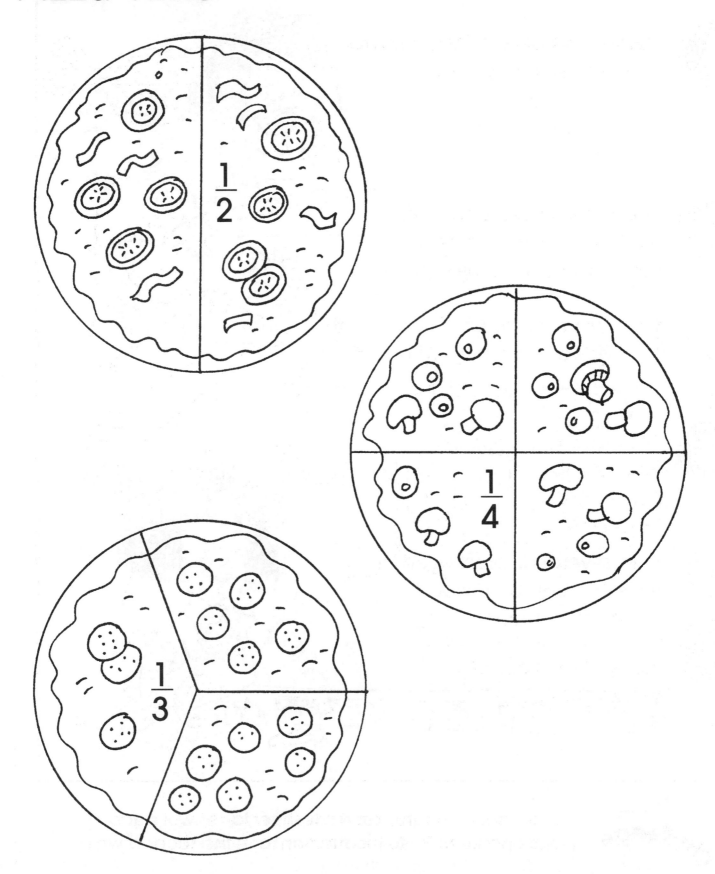

Fractions

Walls

1 Use linking cubes to build several different-sized walls that can be divided into halves (2 equal parts).

2 Build several different-sized walls that can be divided into fourths (4 equal parts).

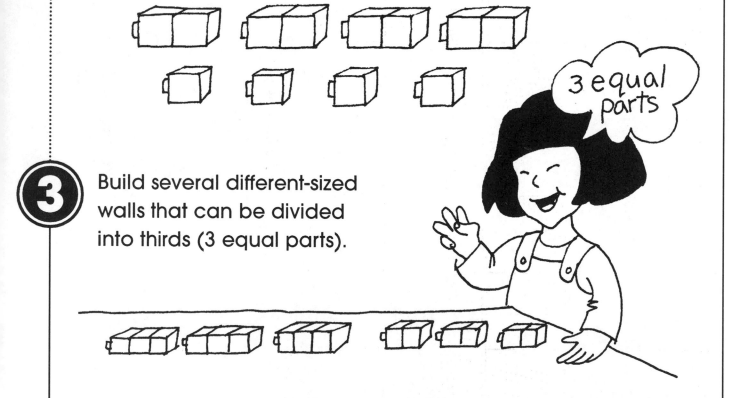

3 Build several different-sized walls that can be divided into thirds (3 equal parts).

Challenge

Color the cubes on your Walls sheet to show 2 equal parts on the first wall, 4 equal parts on the second wall, and 3 equal parts on the third wall.

Walls

Name _____

Color the cubes to show 2 equal parts (halves). Use 2 different colors.

Color the cubes to show 4 equal parts (fourths). Use 4 different colors.

Color the cubes to show 3 equal parts (thirds). Use 3 different colors.

Instant Math Centers • K–1 © 2000 Creative Teaching Press

Fractions

Geometry

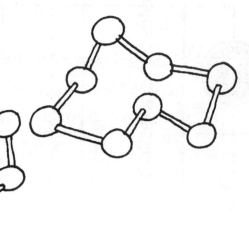

These center activities focus on basic geometric concepts. Students will explore the properties of geometric shapes and create symmetrical designs.

Shape Cover-Up
Teaching Tips and Extensions
- Depending on the ability level of your students, you may want to put out only the four pattern block shapes outlined on the activity sheet.

Materials
- ☐ Shape Cover-Up reproducibles (pages 51–52)
- ☐ pattern blocks

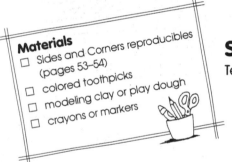

Materials
- ☐ Sides and Corners reproducibles (pages 53–54)
- ☐ colored toothpicks
- ☐ modeling clay or play dough
- ☐ crayons or markers

Sides and Corners
Teaching Tips and Extensions
- Show students how to use the clay and toothpicks to construct shapes. Mini-marshmallows can also be used instead of clay.
- Use straws or pipe cleaners in place of the toothpicks. If you vary the length of these items, students can construct a greater variety of shapes.

Symmetrical Designs
Teaching Tips and Extensions
- Discuss the meaning of *symmetry*.
- If you do not have colored tiles, cut red, blue, yellow, and green construction paper in 1" (2.5 cm) squares. Students could glue these on the Graph Paper (page 56) for the Challenge activity instead of coloring in the squares.

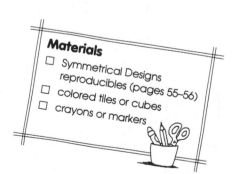

Materials
- ☐ Symmetrical Designs reproducibles (pages 55–56)
- ☐ colored tiles or cubes
- ☐ crayons or markers

Shape Cover-Up

1 Use pattern blocks to completely cover the triangle shape on your Shape Cover-Up sheet.

2 Use tally marks to record how many of each shape you used. Write the total number of shapes used.

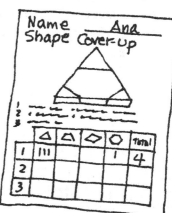

3 Repeat the activity 2 more times. Use a different combination of pattern blocks each time.

Challenge Use pattern blocks to build the triangle without using the Shape Cover-Up sheet as a pattern. Can you make a bigger or smaller triangle?

Geometry

Instant Math Centers • K-1 © 2000 Creative Teaching Press

Shape Cover-Up

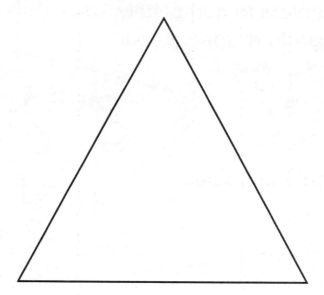

1. Use pattern blocks to cover the triangle. Do it 3 different ways.

2. Use tally marks to record how many of each shape you used.

3. Write the total number of shapes used for each try.

	△	⬠	▱	⬡	Total
1					
2					
3					

Sides and Corners

 Use the toothpicks and clay to build a shape with 3 sides and 3 corners.

 Build a shape with 4 sides and 4 corners.

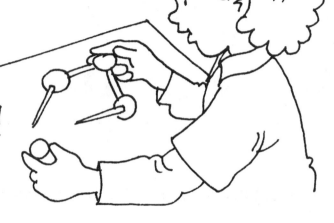

 Build a shape with 5 sides and 5 corners.

4 Build some shapes with more than 5 sides and 5 corners.

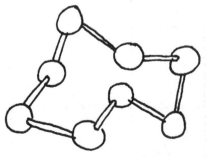

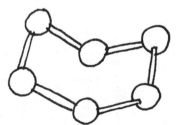

 Draw several of your shapes on your journal page. Write the number of sides and corners for each shape.

Geometry

Math Journal

Draw several of your clay and toothpick shapes.
Write the number of sides and corners for each
shape.

Symmetrical Designs

1 Work with a partner. Use colored tiles or cubes to build a design on 1 side of a Graph Paper sheet. Start the design on the center line.

2 Invite your partner to build a symmetrical design on the other side of the center line.

3 Switch roles and repeat the activity several times.

Copy and color 1 of your symmetrical designs on another Graph Paper sheet.

Instant Math Centers • K–1 © 2000 Creative Teaching Press

Geometry

Graph Paper

Name _____

Instant Math Centers • K-1 © 2000 Creative Teaching Press

Graphing

Learning how to make and read graphs is an important problem-solving skill. Concrete graphs, which compare quantities of real things, are most easily understood by young students. Picture graphs connect the real to the abstract and prepare students for the introduction of symbolic graphs, which use symbols, such as letters, numbers, lines, or bars, to display information.

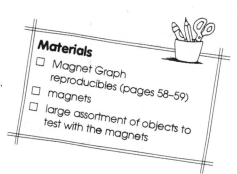

Magnet Graph
Teaching Tips and Extensions

- Photocopy a few copies of the Magnet Graph on tagboard, and laminate them.
- Encourage students to bring in objects to test with the magnet.

Materials
- ☐ Magnet Graph reproducibles (pages 58–59)
- ☐ magnets
- ☐ large assortment of objects to test with the magnets

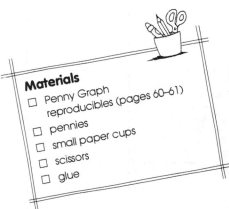

Materials
- ☐ Penny Graph reproducibles (pages 60–61)
- ☐ pennies
- ☐ small paper cups
- ☐ scissors
- ☐ glue

Penny Graph
Teaching Tips and Extensions

- ☆ After photocopying the Penny Graph, cut apart the two sections before placing them at the center.
- Ask students *Did you roll more "heads" or "tails"?* Use their responses to make a class graph.

M&M Graph
Teaching Tips and Extensions

- Before photocopying the graph, check the colors of the M&M candies you purchased. The color assortment can sometimes vary.
- Substitute small bags of jelly beans or trail mix for the M&M's.
- Ask students *What color were most of your candies?* Use their responses to make a class graph.

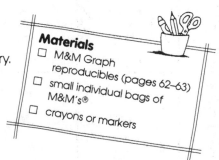

Materials
- ☐ M&M Graph reproducibles (pages 62–63)
- ☐ small individual bags of M&M's®
- ☐ crayons or markers

Magnet Graph

1 Test each object to see if the magnet can pick it up.

2 Place each object on the correct side of your Magnet Graph.

3 Tell a classmate about your graph.

Challenge Draw a picture and write the names of the objects on each side of your Magnet Graph.

Name _____

Magnet Graph

Can a magnet pick it up?	
Yes	No

Graphing

Penny Graph

1 Shake 1 penny in a paper cup and then pour it out.

2 If the penny lands "heads up," put it in the heads row of your Penny Graph. If it lands "tails up," put it in the tails row.

3 Repeat the activity with 9 more pennies.

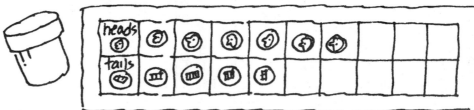

4 Make a picture graph by cutting apart the paper pennies and gluing them on your Penny Graph in place of the real pennies.

 Repeat the activity. Compare your results and tell a classmate how your graph changed.

Instant Math Centers • K–1 © 2000 Creative Teaching Press

Penny Graph

Name _____

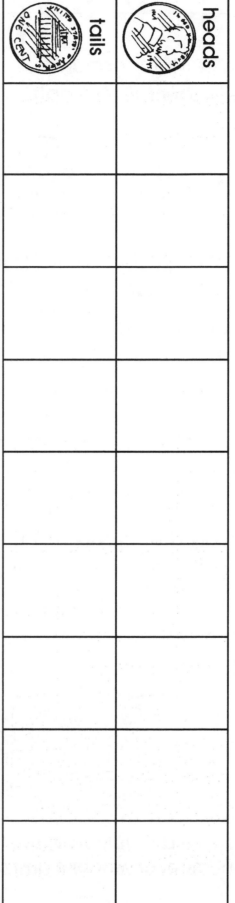

	heads								
	tails								

Graphing

M&M Graph

1 Sort 1 bag of M&M® candies by color on your M&M Graph.

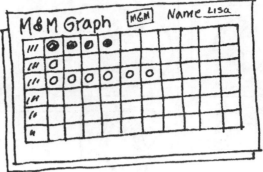

2 Then take off the M&M's one at a time and color each box to match the candy.

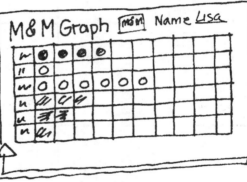

3 Count the M&M's in each row and record how many there are of each color. Tell a classmate about your graph.

Challenge Make a graph on a sheet of paper, showing the number of windows and doors in your classroom.

Instant Math Centers • K–1 © 2000 Creative Teaching Press

M&M Graph

Name _____

orange									
brown									
yellow									
green									
red									
blue									

I had _____ orange   _____ green   _____ yellow

        _____ brown   _____ red   **Total Number**

        _____ yellow   _____ blue   _____

Instant Math Centers • K–1 © 2000 Creative Teaching Press

Graphing

Measurement

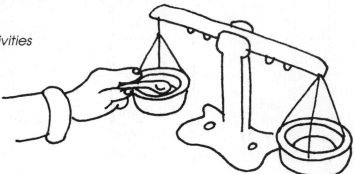

Students will enjoy these exploratory center activities as they estimate, measure, and compare, using a variety of nonstandard units of measurement. These activities offer students experiences in measuring capacity, length, and weight.

How Many Cubes?
Teaching Tips and Extensions
- Discuss the meaning of *capacity.*
- For first experiences with measuring capacity, keep the containers small. Increase the size as students become more proficient at estimating and measuring.
- Encourage students to fill the container half full and then revise their estimate, if necessary.

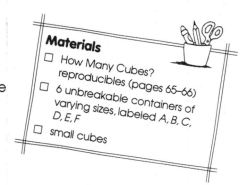

Materials
- ☐ How Many Cubes? reproducibles (pages 65–66)
- ☐ 6 unbreakable containers of varying sizes, labeled A, B, C, D, E, F
- ☐ small cubes

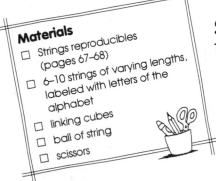

Materials
- ☐ Strings reproducibles (pages 67–68)
- ☐ 6–10 strings of varying lengths, labeled with letters of the alphabet
- ☐ linking cubes
- ☐ ball of string
- ☐ scissors

Strings
Teaching Tips and Extensions
- Have students estimate the length of each string before measuring it.
- Have students use different-colored yarns and ribbons as well as string.

Inchworms to Inches
Teaching Tips and Extensions
- Introduce the activity by reading aloud *Inch by Inch* by Leo Lionni.
- Remind students that the inchworms must be glued down end-to-end for accuracy in measuring.
- For fun, have students measure licorice and then eat it.

Materials
- ☐ Inchworms to Inches reproducibles (pages 69–70)
- ☐ scissors
- ☐ construction paper
- ☐ glue

Materials
- ☐ Guess and Weigh reproducibles (pages 71–72)
- ☐ assorted small objects to weigh (e.g., box of crayons, toy cars, blocks, pinecones)
- ☐ 2–3 balance scales
- ☐ small cubes

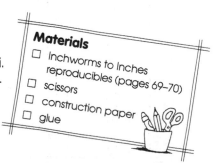

Guess and Weigh
Teaching Tips and Extensions
- Have students work in pairs.
- Encourage students to bring their own objects to weigh.
- Be sure the selected objects are not too heavy for the nonstandard units of measurement being used.

How Many Cubes?

1 Pick 1 container. Guess how many cubes will fill it up.

2 Write your guess on your How Many Cubes? sheet.

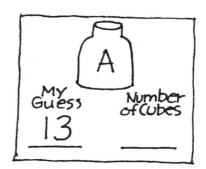

3 Fill the container with cubes. Then empty the container and count the cubes.

4 Write the number of cubes on your sheet. Repeat the activity with 5 more containers.

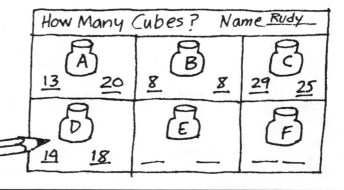

Arrange the containers from smallest to largest capacity.

Instant Math Centers • K–1 © 2000 Creative Teaching Press

Measurement

How Many Cubes?

A	B	C
My Guess ____	My Guess ____	My Guess ____
Number of Cubes ____	Number of Cubes ____	Number of Cubes ____

D	E	F
My Guess ____	My Guess ____	My Guess ____
Number of Cubes ____	Number of Cubes ____	Number of Cubes ____

Instant Math Centers • K–1 © 2000 Creative Teaching Press

Strings

1 Choose 1 string. Write its letter on your Strings sheet.

2 Line up linking cubes along the string. Write the number of cubes on your sheet.

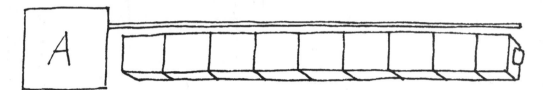

3 Repeat the activity with 5 more strings.

Challenge Work with a partner to measure your height with string. Then count how many cubes tall you are and write the number on your sheet.

Measurement

Name _____

Strings

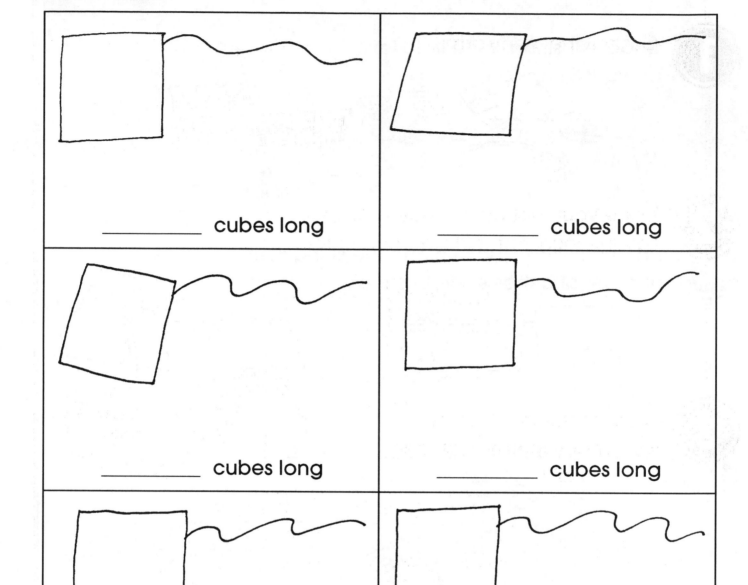

_____ cubes long

_____ cubes long

_____ cubes long

_____ cubes long

_____ cubes long

_____ cubes long

I am _____ cubes tall.

Inchworms to Inches

1 Cut out the inchworms.

2 Trace your foot on a piece of paper.
Lay the inchworms down the center.

3 Glue on the inchworms.
How many inchworms long
is your foot?

6 inchworms long.

4 Trace your hand and
repeat the measuring
activity.

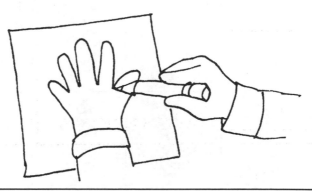

Challenge Find something in your classroom that is the same length
as your hand or foot.

Measurement

Inchworms

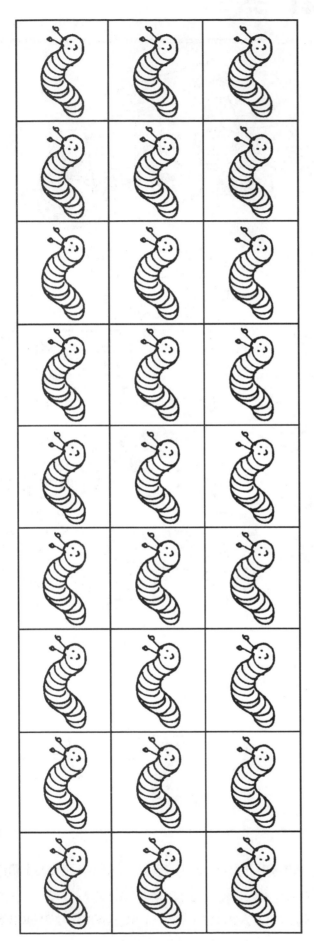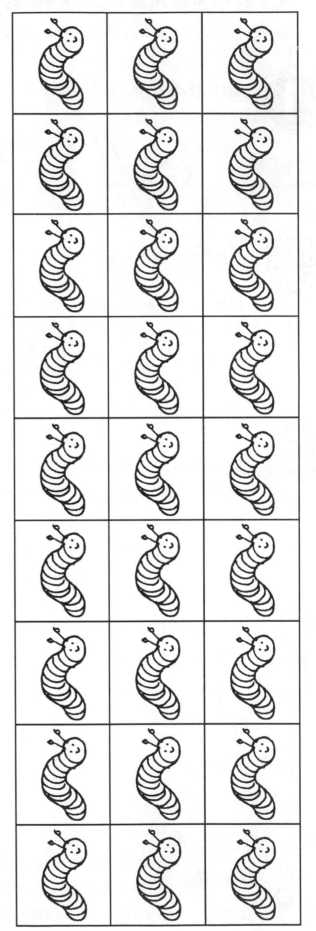

Guess and Weigh

1 Choose 1 object. Put it on the scale.

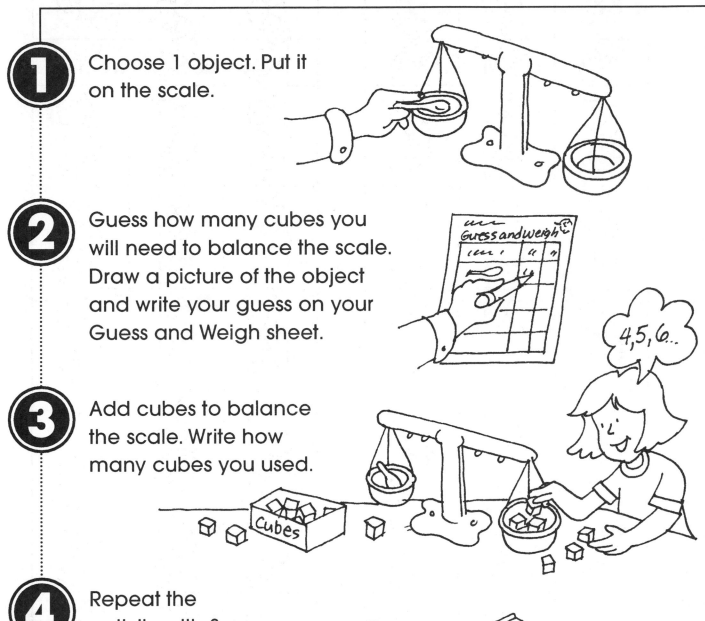

2 Guess how many cubes you will need to balance the scale. Draw a picture of the object and write your guess on your Guess and Weigh sheet.

3 Add cubes to balance the scale. Write how many cubes you used.

4 Repeat the activity with 3 other objects.

Challenge Put the 4 objects you weighed in order from lightest to heaviest. Choose 5 more objects to weigh on the balance scale. Put them in order from lightest to heaviest.

Measurement

Guess and Weigh

What I Weighed	My Guess	Weight

Money

Your students will have fun learning about money as they work with these center activities. The focus is to help students identify and learn the value of a penny, nickel, dime, and quarter. Students will benefit most from these activities by using real coins as they work.

Graphing Coins
Teaching Tips and Extensions

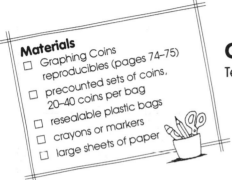

Materials
- ☐ Graphing Coins reproducibles (pages 74–75)
- ☐ precounted sets of coins, 20–40 coins per bag
- ☐ resealable plastic bags
- ☐ crayons or markers
- ☐ large sheets of paper

- Vary the number and type of coins in each bag to make each graph different.
- Have students use coin stamps, instead of drawing circles, to represent coins on their graph.
- Store each set of coins in a piggy bank instead of a plastic bag. Look for "openable" piggy banks at garage sales and thrift stores.

Money Count
Teaching Tips and Extensions

- Vary the number and type of coins in the bags according to the ability levels of your students.
- Provide paper coins or coin stamps so students can record the amount in each bag.

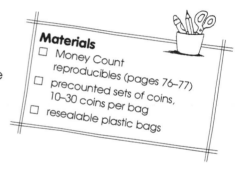

Materials
- ☐ Money Count reproducibles (pages 76–77)
- ☐ precounted sets of coins, 10–30 coins per bag
- ☐ resealable plastic bags

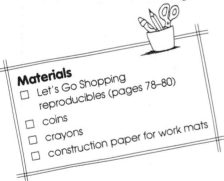

Materials
- ☐ Let's Go Shopping reproducibles (pages 78–80)
- ☐ coins
- ☐ crayons
- ☐ construction paper for work mats

Let's Go Shopping
Teaching Tips and Extensions

- ☆ Add prices to the Picture Cards before photocopying them and cutting them apart.
- Vary the prices on the Picture Cards according to the ability levels of your students.
- Laminate several sets of Picture Cards.
- Place price tags on small objects instead of using the Picture Cards reproducible.
- Have students work in pairs, buying items and making change.

Money Combinations
Teaching Tips and Extensions

- ☆ Add prices to the Picture Cards before photocopying them and cutting them apart.
- Vary the prices on the Picture Cards according to the ability levels of your students.
- Laminate several sets of Picture Cards.
- Introduce the activity with the book *26 Letters and 99 Cents* by Tana Hoban.

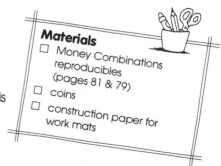

Materials
- ☐ Money Combinations reproducibles (pages 81 & 79)
- ☐ coins
- ☐ construction paper for work mats

Graphing Coins

1 Sort 1 bag of coins by value and lay the coins on the table in rows to form a graph.

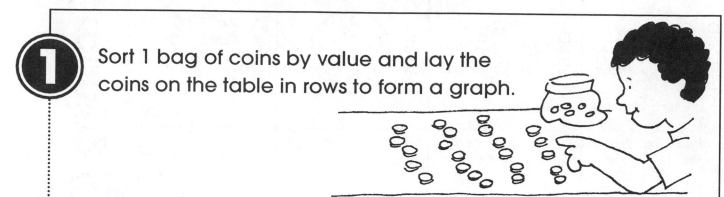

2 Count the number of pennies. Draw that many circles next to the penny on your Graphing Coins sheet.

3 Do the same for the nickels, dimes, and quarters.

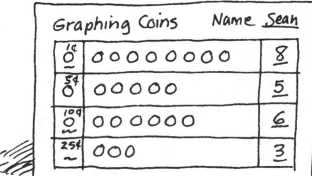

Graphing Coins		Name _Sean_
1¢ O	O O O O O O O O	8
5¢ O	O O O O O	5
10¢ O	O O O O O O	6
25¢	O O O	3

4 Count the coins in each row. Write the total number of coins in each row on your sheet.

 With a classmate, use two bags of coins to form a larger graph. Copy the graph on a large sheet of paper.

Instant Math Centers • K–1 © 2000 Creative Teaching Press

Graphing Coins

Name _____

1¢ pennies	How many?
5¢ nickels	How many?
10¢ dimes	How many?
25¢ quarters	How many?

Instant Math Centers • K–1 © 2000 Creative Teaching Press

Money

Money Count

1 Sort 1 bag of coins by value. Count the number of each coin, and make a tally mark for each coin on your Money Recording Sheet.

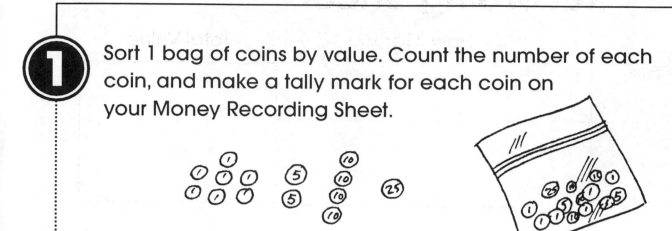

2 Find the total value for each type of coin. (Example: 3 nickels = 15¢)

2 nickels are 10 cents, 4 dimes are 40 cents.

3 Write each amount on your sheet.

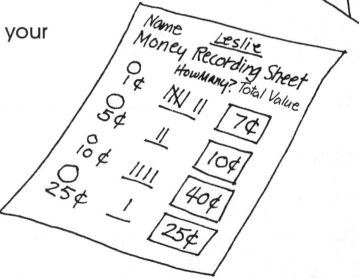

Choose 2 bags of coins. Find the total value in both bags.

Instant Math Centers • K–1 © 2000 Creative Teaching Press

Name_____

Money Recording Sheet

How Many?   Total Value

1¢   _____

5¢   _____

10¢   _____

25¢   _____

Instant Math Centers • K-1 © 2000 Creative Teaching Press

Money

Let's Go Shopping

1 Stack the picture cards facedown.
Turn over 2 cards.

2 Show the coins needed to buy each item.

3 Tell a classmate how much it would cost to
buy both items.

4 Repeat the activity with different picture cards.

Math Journal Draw your own picture card on your journal page. Put a
price on the card. Show the coins needed to buy the item.

Picture Cards

Directions: Add prices before reproducing these cards.

airplane	cookie	soccer ball
book	pencil	grapes
yo-yo	ice cream	bear
bubbles	necklace	baseball bat

Money

Math Journal

Draw your own picture card. Put a price on the card. Show the coins needed to buy the item.

Money Combinations

1 Stack the picture cards facedown. Turn over 1 card.

2 Find several different ways to use the coins to match the price on the picture card.

3 Choose new picture cards and repeat the activity.

 **Challenge** Add together the prices on 2 picture cards. Show different combinations of coins to equal that amount.

Money

Patterns

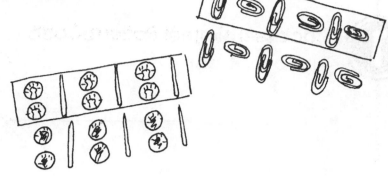

The study of mathematics involves the ability to recognize and analyze underlying patterns. Students need repeated opportunities to identify, reproduce, and create patterns. These experiences should be hands-on and appropriate to the needs of your students.

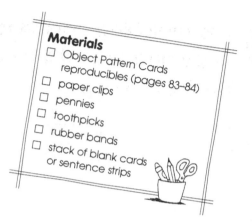

Object Pattern Cards

Teaching Tips and Extensions

☆ Photocopy, cut apart, and laminate the Object Pattern Cards.

● Introduce the activity by reading aloud *Look Again* by Tana Hoban.

Materials
- ☐ Object Pattern Cards reproducibles (pages 83–84)
- ☐ paper clips
- ☐ pennies
- ☐ toothpicks
- ☐ rubber bands
- ☐ stack of blank cards or sentence strips

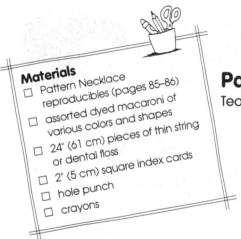

Materials
- ☐ Pattern Necklace reproducibles (pages 85–86)
- ☐ assorted dyed macaroni of various colors and shapes
- ☐ 24" (61 cm) pieces of thin string or dental floss
- ☐ 2" (5 cm) square index cards
- ☐ hole punch
- ☐ crayons

Pattern Necklace

Teaching Tips and Extensions

☆ Punch a hole in each index card. Tie each piece of string or floss to the card so the macaroni cannot slip off the end.

● To dye macaroni, place it in a bowl or resealable bag with a few tablespoons of rubbing alcohol and several drops of food coloring. Drain and dry overnight.

Place Mat Patterns

Teaching Tips and Extensions

● You may want to tell students to color all the bananas yellow, all the apples red, and all the grapes green. This would eliminate color as a variable in the pattern.

● Pattern Homework: Look at home for a pattern on place mats, tablecloths, or dishes. Copy the pattern and bring it to class.

Materials
- ☐ Place Mat Patterns reproducibles (pages 87–89)
- ☐ crayons or markers
- ☐ scissors
- ☐ 12" x 18" (30.5 cm x 46 cm) colored construction paper
- ☐ glue

Object Pattern Cards

1 Choose 1 Object Pattern Card.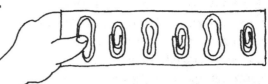

2 Use matching objects to copy and extend the pattern on the card.

3 Say your pattern out loud.

Rubber band, paper clip, rubber band, paper clip....

4 Copy and extend the patterns on at least 3 different cards.

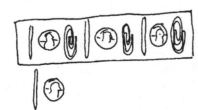 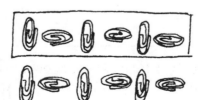 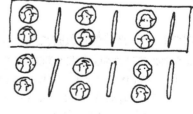

Challenge Create your own pattern on a blank card. Give it to a classmate to copy and extend.

Patterns

Object Pattern Cards

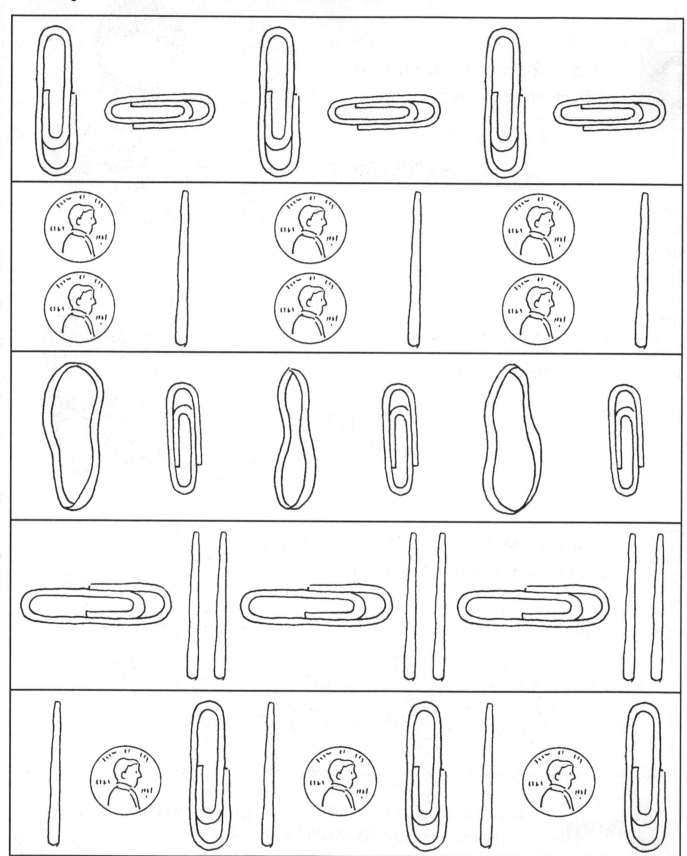

Pattern Necklace

1 Choose 2 different colors or shapes of macaroni.

2 String the macaroni onto a necklace in a pattern.

3 Use crayons to copy your pattern on your Pattern Necklace sheet.

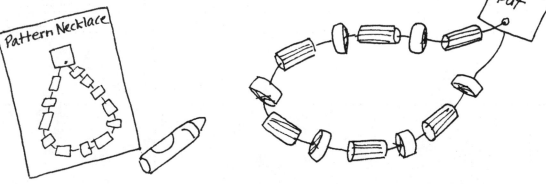

 Use 3 or 4 different colors or shapes to make a new macaroni pattern necklace.

Patterns

Pattern Necklace

Draw a picture of your macaroni pattern necklace.

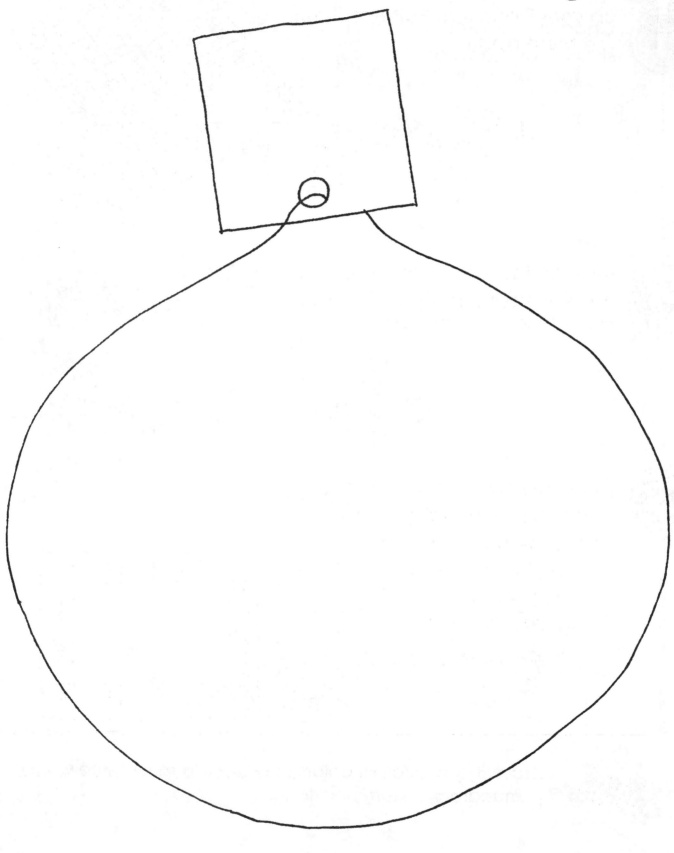

Place Mat Patterns

1 Color the apples, bananas, and grapes on your Place Mat Patterns sheet. Cut them apart.

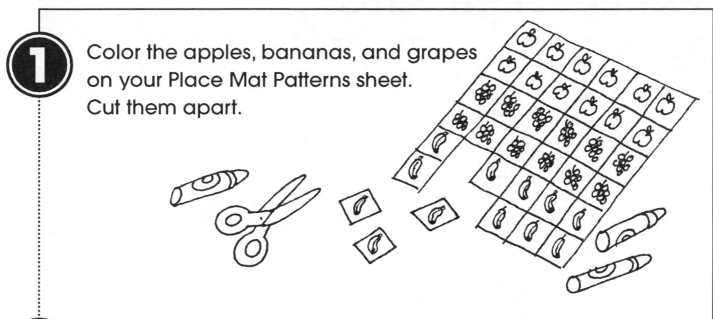

2 Arrange the fruit to form a pattern around the edge of your construction paper.

3 Glue the pattern in place to create a place mat. Then read your pattern to a partner.

Apple, apple grapes, apple.

 **Math Journal** Draw a food pattern around the edge of the plate on your journal page.

Place Mat Patterns

88

Name _____

Math Journal

Draw a food pattern around the edge of this plate.

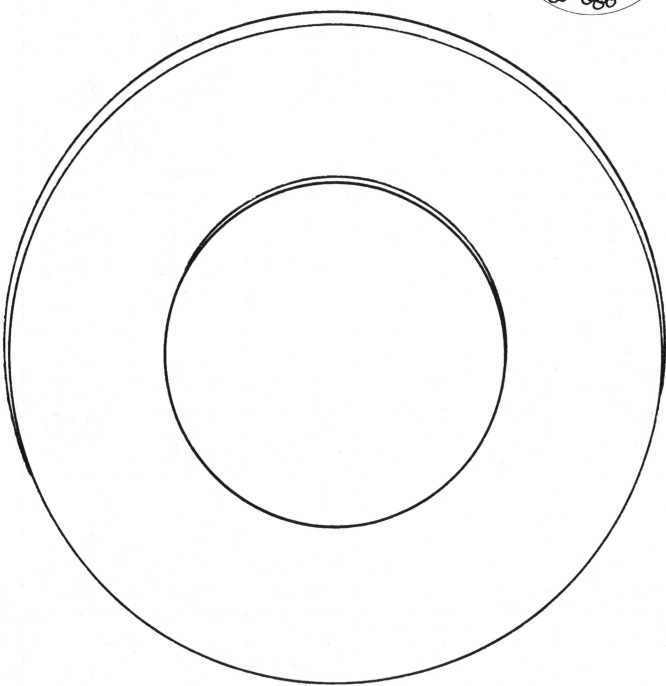

Patterns

Place Value

To understand the concept of place value, students
will need many experiences counting and grouping
concrete objects into sets of ten. Vary the manipulatives
and activities (e.g., counting beans into cups, linking
cubes into groups of ten, bundling straws into groups
of ten). As students become more confident in their
ability to group and count by tens, they can move
on to recording tens and ones.

Place Value Counting Jars
Teaching Tips and Extensions

- Vary the number of objects in each jar according to the ability
  levels of your students. Objects should be small enough to fit at
  least ten in one cup.
- Invite students to bring objects from home to fill a jar.

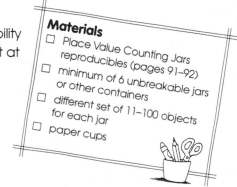

Materials
- ☐ Place Value Counting Jars reproducibles (pages 91–92)
- ☐ minimum of 6 unbreakable jars or other containers
- ☐ different set of 11–100 objects for each jar
- ☐ paper cups

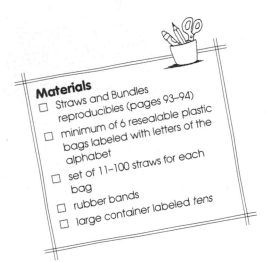

Materials
- ☐ Straws and Bundles reproducibles (pages 93–94)
- ☐ minimum of 6 resealable plastic bags labeled with letters of the alphabet
- ☐ set of 11–100 straws for each bag
- ☐ rubber bands
- ☐ large container labeled tens

Straws and Bundles
Teaching Tips and Extensions

- Have students choose a teacher-made number card
  between 11 and 99 and bundle straws to match that
  number.
- Place a larger container marked *hundreds* at the center
  for students who count beyond 100 straws.
- Use craft sticks instead of straws.

Place Value Hopscotch
Teaching Tips and Extensions

- Have students color sets of ten squares on a sheet of graph
  paper to record the number of cubes they counted.
- Draw a large hopscotch pattern on butcher paper or outdoors
  on the sidewalk. Play the game outdoors as a class.

Materials
- ☐ Place Value Hopscotch reproducibles (pages 95–96 & 94)
- ☐ counters to toss onto hopscotch game board
- ☐ linking cubes in assorted colors

Place Value Counting Jars

1 Choose 1 jar of objects and 10 cups.

2 Count the objects by tens into the cups.

3 Count by tens and ones to find the total number of objects.

10, 20, 30...
31, 32

4 Repeat the activity with other jars.

Math Journal

Draw a picture on your journal page that shows how you grouped the objects in one of the jars by tens and ones. Write the total number.

Place Value

Name _____

Math Journal

Draw a picture that shows how you grouped the objects in one of the jars by tens and ones. Write the total number.

Instant Math Centers • K–1 © 2000 Creative Teaching Press

Straws and Bundles

1 Sort 1 bag of straws into groups of 10. Wrap each group with a rubber band.

2 Place the bundles in the tens container. Count by tens and ones to find the total number of straws.

10, 20, 30... 31, 32

3 Repeat the activity with 5 more bags of straws.

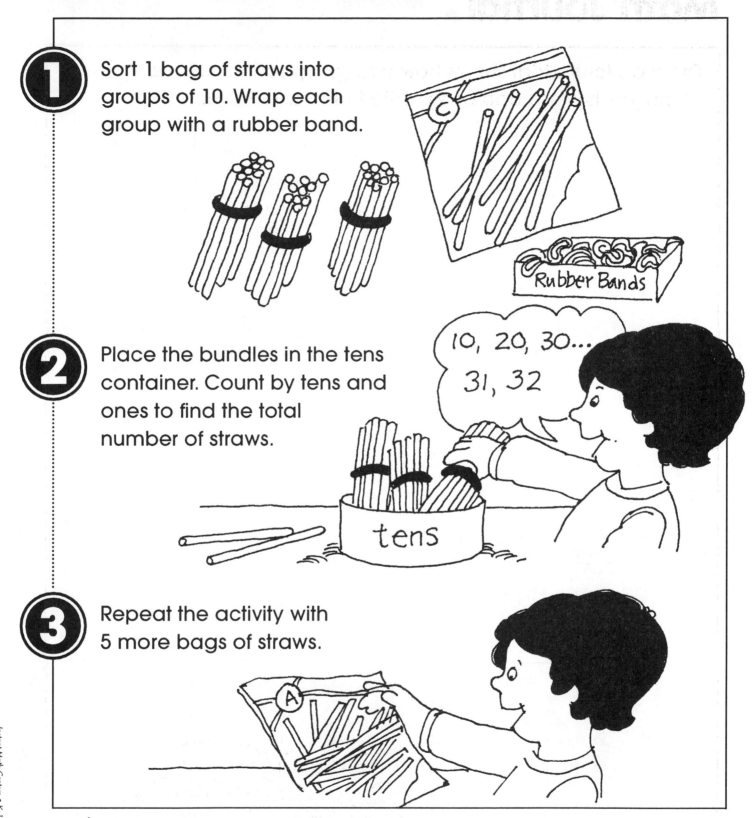

Challenge Write the number of straws in each bag on your Tens and Ones sheet.

Place Value

Tens and Ones

10s	1s
tens	ones

10s	1s
tens	ones

10s	1s
tens	ones

10s	1s
tens	ones

10s	1s
tens	ones

10s	1s
tens	ones

Instant Math Centers • K–1 © 2000 Creative Teaching Press

Place Value Hopscotch

1 Toss 2 counters onto your hopscotch game board. Write 1 number in the tens box and write the other in the ones box on your Tens and Ones sheet.

2 Build that number with linking cubes. Group the cubes by tens and ones.

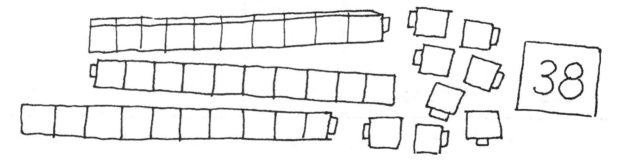

3 Repeat the activity 5 more times, writing the 2 numbers each time.

Play the game with a partner. Compare your numbers after each toss. Who has the bigger number?

Instant Math Centers • K–1 © 2000 Creative Teaching Press

Place Value

Place Value Hopscotch

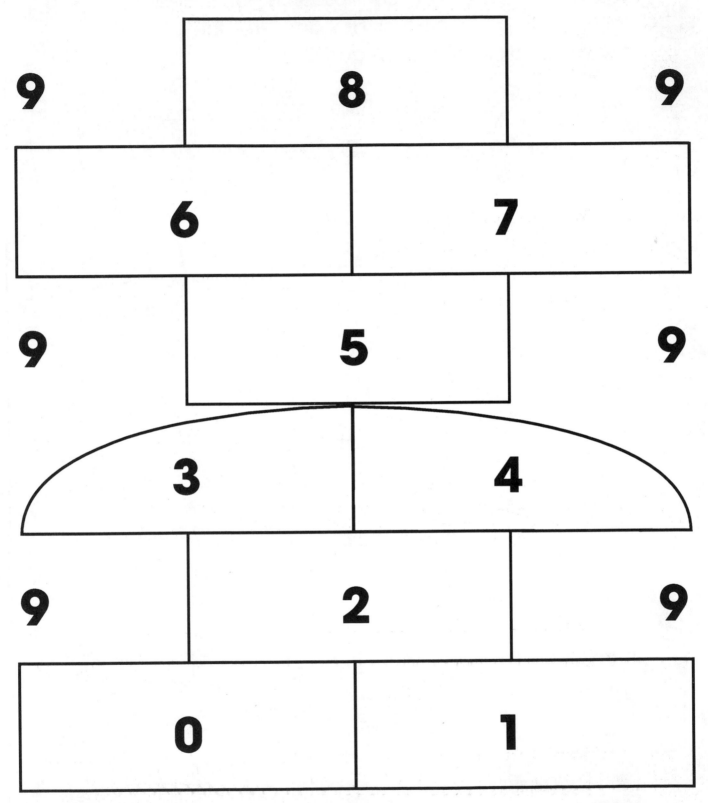

Shapes

In the early-childhood study of geometry, students investigate two- and three-dimensional space and begin to make mathematical connections to the world around them. As students work with these activities, they will explore, sort, and label different shapes and figures.

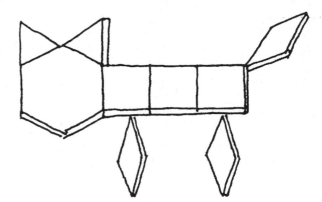

Sorting Shapes
Teaching Tips and Extensions

☆ Photocopy the Shape Patterns on colored construction paper. Cut out the shapes, and put one set in each bag. Mix the colors.

● Use attribute blocks instead of the paper shapes.

● For a snack, serve students crackers shaped like circles, squares, triangles, and rectangles.

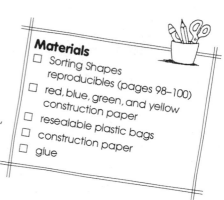

Materials
- ☐ Sorting Shapes reproducibles (pages 98–100)
- ☐ red, blue, green, and yellow construction paper
- ☐ resealable plastic bags
- ☐ construction paper
- ☐ glue

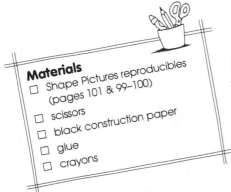

Materials
- ☐ Shape Pictures reproducibles (pages 101 & 99–100)
- ☐ scissors
- ☐ black construction paper
- ☐ glue
- ☐ crayons

Shape Pictures
Teaching Tips and Extensions

● Photocopy extra copies of the Shape Patterns for the Challenge activity.

● You may want to precut the shapes.

● Introduce the activity by reading aloud *Let's Look for Shapes* by Bill Gillham.

Shape Animals
Teaching Tips and Extensions

● Introduce the activity by reading aloud *Color Farm* or *Color Zoo* by Lois Ehlert.

● Make giant-sized pattern blocks out of poster board. Let students form giant shape animals on the floor.

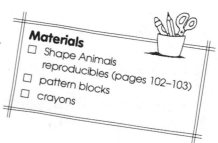

Materials
- ☐ Shape Animals reproducibles (pages 102–103)
- ☐ pattern blocks
- ☐ crayons

Sorting Shapes

1 Work with a partner.
Take 1 bag of shapes.

2 Sort all the triangles, circles, squares, and rectangles.

3 Sort them again in different ways.

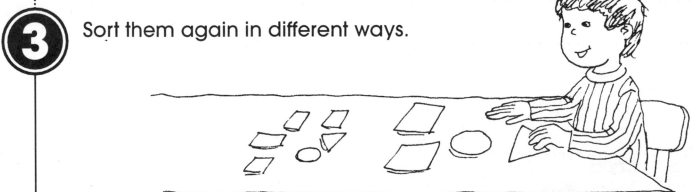

Challenge Glue the shapes on a piece of paper to show one way you sorted them. Label each shape.

Shape Patterns (A)

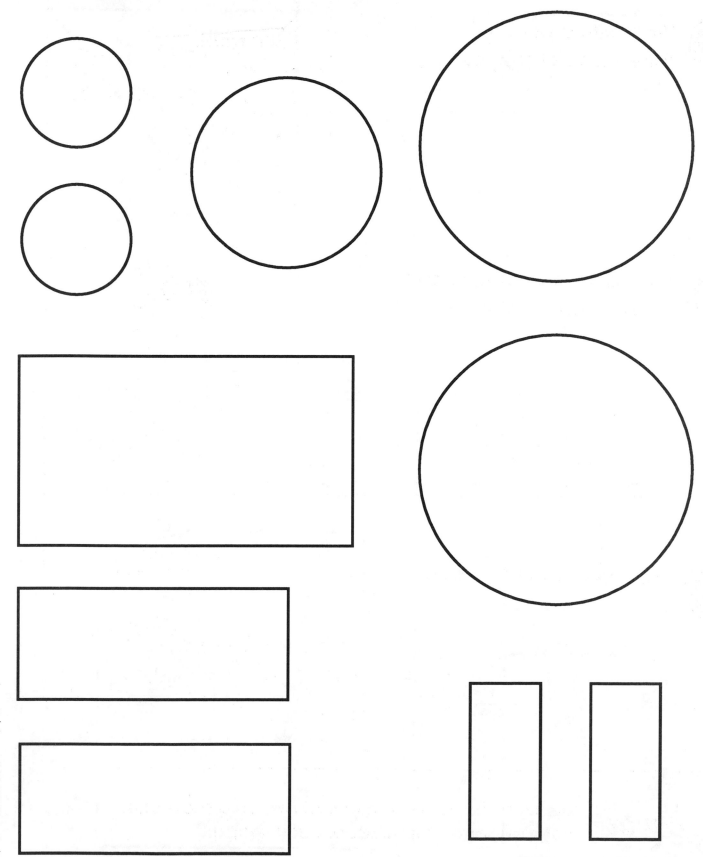

Shapes

Shape Patterns (B)

Instant Math Centers • K–1 © 2000 Creative Teaching Press

Shape Pictures

1 Cut out the shapes.

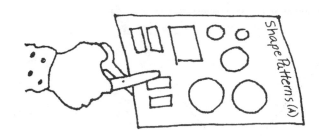

2 Move the shape pieces around to make a scene on the black paper.

3 Glue your shape scene on the paper. Add details with crayons.

4 Tell a classmate about your shape picture.

 **Challenge** Work with a partner to use 2 sets of shapes to create a larger shape picture.

Instant! Math Centers • K–1 © 2000 Creative Teaching Press

Shapes

Shape Animals

1 Use pattern blocks to make a pet cat like this one.

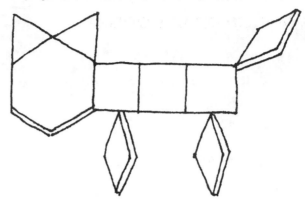

2 Use pattern blocks to make a wild lion.

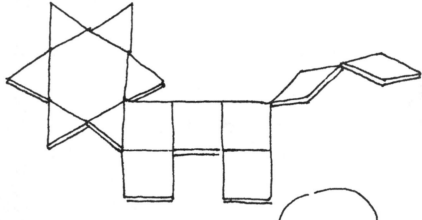

3 Use pattern blocks to make at least 4 different animals.

Math Journal

Trace around the blocks you used for 1 shape animal on your journal page. Color in your drawing.

Instant Math Centers • K–1 © 2000 Creative Teaching Press

Math Journal

Trace around the blocks you used for
1 shape animal on this page.

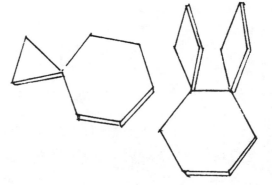

Instant Math Centers • K–1 © 2000 Creative Teaching Press

Sorting and Classifying

Sorting and classifying activities encourage students to be more aware and accurate in their observation of the world around them and help them to think in an analytical manner in problem-solving situations. Encourage students to look for a wide variety of attributes (same or different) for any given set of objects in these center activities.

Sorting Beans
Teaching Tips and Extensions

- Laminate several Bean Sorting Mats.
- Have students list different categories for sorting beans.
- For delicious fun, prepare bean soup or bean salad (or both) with your class!

Materials
- ☐ Sorting Beans reproducibles (pages 105–106)
- ☐ dried beans in assorted colors
- ☐ container for beans
- ☐ glue

Materials
- ☐ Sorting Animals reproducibles (pages 107–108)
- ☐ scissors
- ☐ glue
- ☐ construction paper
- ☐ index cards

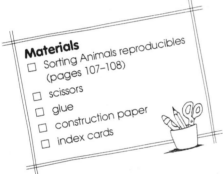

Sorting Animals
Teaching Tips and Extensions

- Have students color individual sets of cards before they cut them apart.
- Prepare several laminated sets of cards to place at the center.
- For fun, have students sort and eat animal crackers.

Snack Sort
Teaching Tips and Extensions

- ☆ Place a mixture of edible items in each cup.
- As a group, brainstorm possible sorting categories. List these on a chart, and place it at the center.
- Invite students to eat the snack food when they have completed the activity.

Materials
- ☐ Snack Sort reproducibles (pages 109–110)
- ☐ cereal, mixed nuts, trail mix, or other snack food items
- ☐ small paper cups
- ☐ crayons or markers

Materials
- ☐ Sorting Words reproducibles (pages 111–112)
- ☐ scissors
- ☐ construction paper
- ☐ glue
- ☐ index cards

Sorting Words
Teaching Tips and Extensions

- Discuss possible attributes to sort by, such as first letter, last letter, number of letters in the word, and words with double letters.
- Have less advanced students sort by picture only.

Sorting Beans

1 Pick a handful of beans.

2 Sort the beans on your Bean Sorting Mat. Can you sort them in different ways?

3 Glue the beans on your sorting mat to show 1 way you sorted them.

Challenge

Have a partner guess your sorting rule.

Sorting and Classifying

Bean Sorting Mat

Instant Math Centers • K–1 © 2000 Creative Teaching Press

Sorting Animals

1 Cut apart the animal cards.

2 Sort the cards in different ways.

3 Glue the cards on a piece of paper to show 1 way you sorted them.

4 Show your paper to a classmate and explain how you sorted the cards.

Challenge Draw a different animal on an index card. Where does it belong on your sorting paper?

Sorting and Classifying

Animal Cards

Instant Math Centers • K–1 © 2000 Creative Teaching Press

Snack Sort

1 Sort 1 cup of snack foods by shape on your Sorting Mat.

2 Sort again, making up your own rule. Tell a classmate your sorting rule.

3 Sort a third way. See if a classmate can guess your sorting rule.

Draw and label each group on your Sorting Mat.

Sorting and Classifying

Name _____

Sorting Mat

110

Sorting Words

1 Cut apart the word cards.

2 Sort the word cards. Tell a classmate your sorting rule.

3 Sort the cards in different ways.

4 Glue the word cards on a piece of paper to show 1 way you sorted them.

Make 3 new word cards. Add them to the sorting groups on your paper.

Sorting and Classifying

Sorting Words

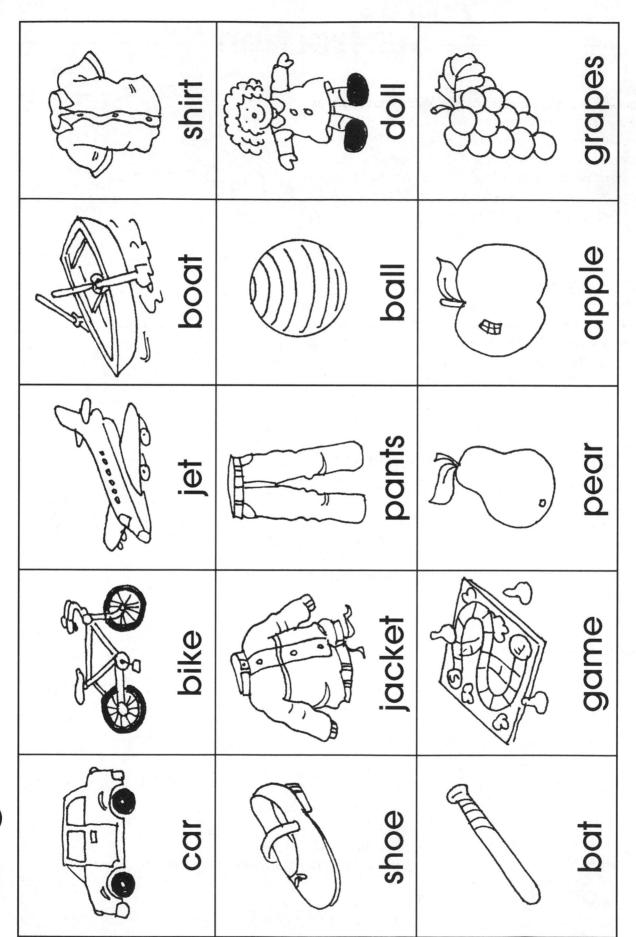

shirt	doll	grapes
boat	ball	apple
jet	pants	pear
bike	jacket	game
car	shoe	bat

Instant Math Centers • K–1 © 2000 Creative Teaching Press

Subtraction

Students will enjoy participating in these math center activities as they improve their subtraction skills. Provide them with a wide variety of manipulatives and many experiences separating sets of objects. As students work and verbalize their findings, they will be ready to record their subtraction equations, first with pictures, and then with number sentences.

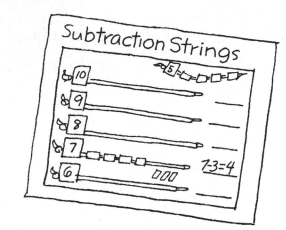

Sand and Sea

Teaching Tips and Extensions

- Laminate several Sand and Sea Work Mats.
- Have students write equations on a sheet of paper as they work.
- Use fish-shaped crackers instead of seashells. Tell story problems as students "catch" fish and eat them.

Materials
- ☐ Sand and Sea reproducibles (pages 114–116)
- ☐ seashell collection or other manipulatives
- ☐ several dice
- ☐ crayons

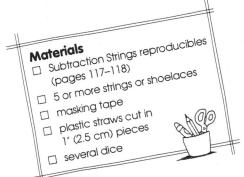

Materials
- ☐ Subtraction Strings reproducibles (pages 117–118)
- ☐ 5 or more strings or shoelaces
- ☐ masking tape
- ☐ plastic straws cut in 1" (2.5 cm) pieces
- ☐ several dice

Subtraction Strings

Teaching Tips and Extensions

- ☆ If you use strings, knot one end and put tape on the other end to make a sharp point. If you use shoelaces, knot them at one end.
- ☆ Write 6, 7, 8, 9, and 10 on pieces of masking tape, and place one piece on each string.

Count and Cover

Teaching Tips and Extensions

- Students can also record their equations by gluing small paper squares or sticking stickers onto a note card and then circling the squares that represent the ones taken away.
- Recite subtraction equations into a tape recorder. Have students "count and cover" blocks for each equation.

Materials
- ☐ Count and Cover reproducible (page 119)
- ☐ blocks or other small manipulatives, bagged in sets of 10
- ☐ resealable plastic bags
- ☐ empty margarine tubs or paper cups
- ☐ paper folded into 8 sections

Materials
- ☐ Dominoes reproducibles (pages 120–121)
- ☐ dominoes
- ☐ beans

Dominoes

Teaching Tips and Extensions

- Make paper dominoes if real ones are not available. Draw dots with a white crayon or paint on black construction paper rectangles.
- Invite each student to place circle stickers on an index card to make an additional domino for the math center.

Sand and Sea

1 Place 6 shells on the sand portion of your Sand and Sea Work Mat.

2 Roll 1 die and "wash" that many shells out to sea. Say a number sentence as you "wash them away."

6 take away 2 is 4.

Sand and Sea Work Mat

3 Play again beginning with 7, then 8, then 9 shells.

4 Play with a classmate. Take turns placing the shells and rolling the die.

Math Journal Write about or draw 1 or more of your seashell subtraction problems on your journal page.

Instant Math Centers • K–1 © 2000 Creative Teaching Press

Sand and Sea Work Mat

Subtraction

Name _____

Math Journal

Write about or draw 1 or more of your seashell subtraction problems.

Instant Math Centers • K–1 © 2000 Creative Teaching Press

Subtraction Strings

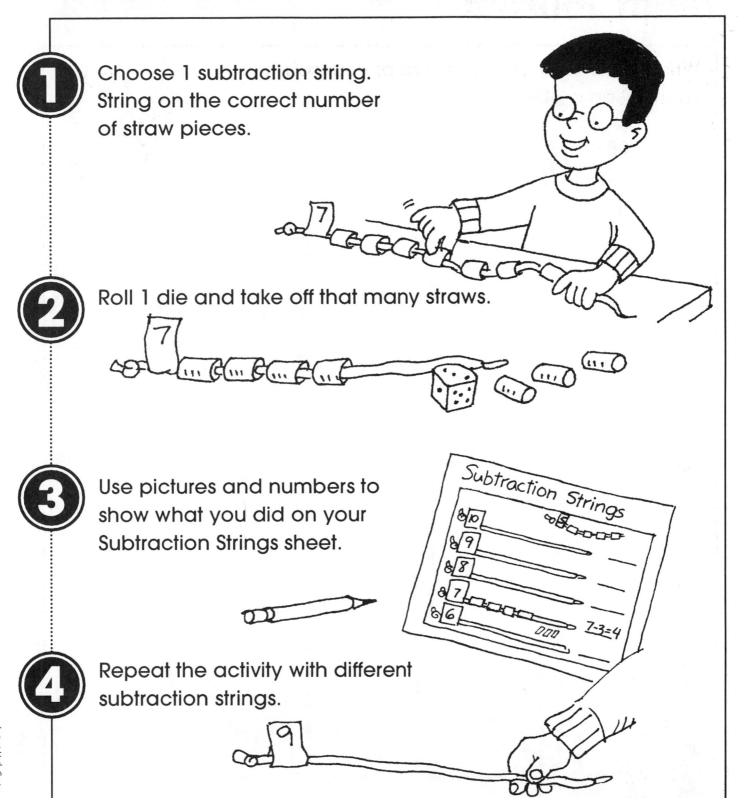

1 Choose 1 subtraction string. String on the correct number of straw pieces.

2 Roll 1 die and take off that many straws.

3 Use pictures and numbers to show what you did on your Subtraction Strings sheet.

4 Repeat the activity with different subtraction strings.

Instant! Math Centers • K-1 © 2000 Creative Teaching Press

Challenge Choose 1 subtraction string. String on the correct number of straw pieces. Write down all the subtraction problems you can think of for that number on the back of your sheet.

Subtraction

Subtraction Strings

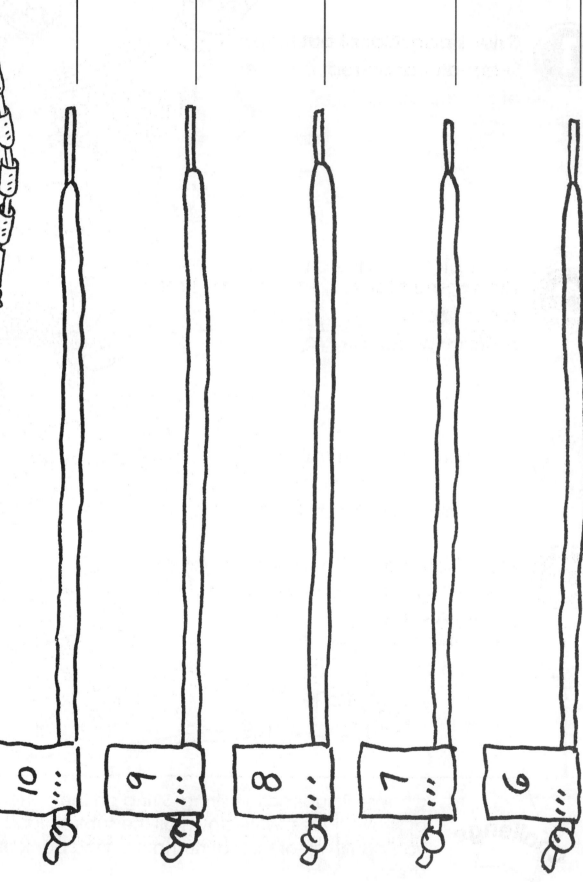

118

Instant Math Centers • K–1 © 2000 Creative Teaching Press

Count and Cover

1 Take 1 bag. Count out a handful of blocks.

2 Hide some blocks under a cup. Write a subtraction number sentence to match on your paper.

5 take away 2 is 3.

5-2=3

3 Play "Count and Cover" 7 more times, beginning with a different number of blocks each time.

5-2=3	6-1=5
8-5=3	4-2=2
2-1=1	3-2=1
9-5=4	7-2=5

Challenge Play "Count and Cover" with a partner. Put both your sets of blocks together to make harder subtraction problems.

Subtraction

Dominoes

 1 Pick 1 domino and make 1 set of beans to match the number of dots on the domino.

2 Cover the dots on 1 side of the domino with your thumb and take away that many beans.

3 As you work, draw the domino and write the matching number sentence on your Dominoes sheet.

4 Repeat the activity with 8 more dominoes.

 **Challenge** Work with a partner. Pick 8 dominoes. Tell a subtraction number sentence and an addition number sentence to match each domino.

Instant Math Centers • K–1 © 2000 Creative Teaching Press

Dominoes

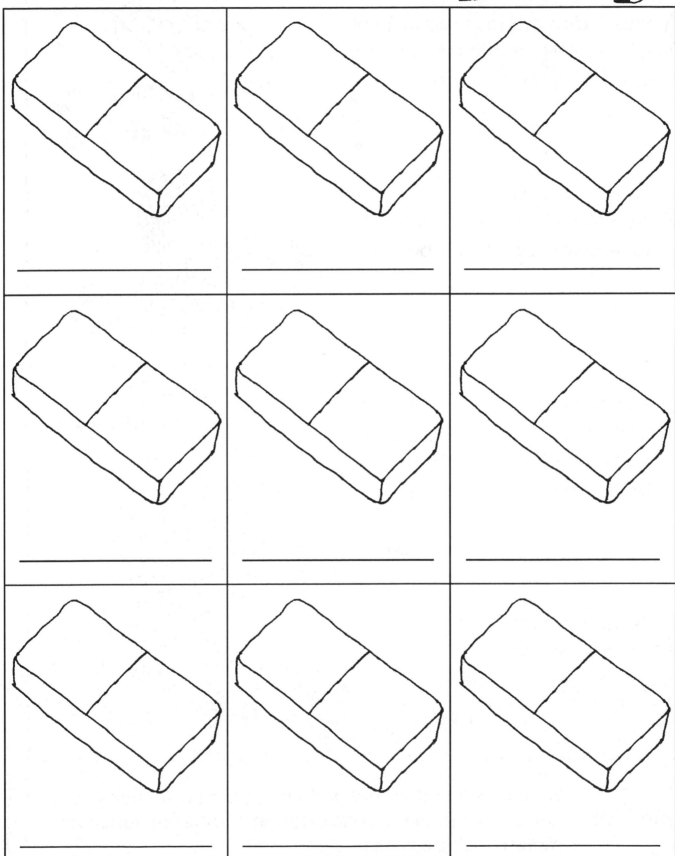

Subtraction

Time

To develop an awareness of time, it is important for young students to participate in activities that focus on sequencing of events and duration of time. Relate these center activities to real-life experiences throughout the school day. Introduce telling time to the hour, using both digital and standard clocks.

Sequence Your Day
Teaching Tips and Extensions

- Introduce the activity by reading aloud *All in a Day* by Mitsumasa Anno.
- Increase the level of difficulty by asking students to sequence five daily activities.

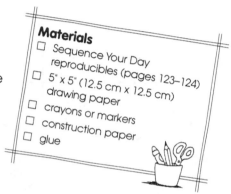

Materials
- [ ] Sequence Your Day reproducibles (pages 123–124)
- [ ] 5" x 5" (12.5 cm x 12.5 cm) drawing paper
- [ ] crayons or markers
- [ ] construction paper
- [ ] glue

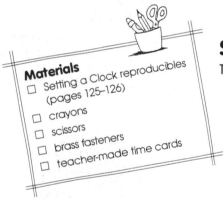

Materials
- [ ] Setting a Clock reproducibles (pages 125–126)
- [ ] crayons
- [ ] scissors
- [ ] brass fasteners
- [ ] teacher-made time cards

Setting a Clock
Teaching Tips and Extensions

- ☆ Photocopy several Clock reproducibles on tagboard. Students may need adult help inserting the brass fastener through the clock hands and face.
- Vary the times on the cards according to the needs of your students.
- For a fun follow-up, have students make edible clock faces with rice cakes, peanut butter, raisins for number dots, and carrot slivers for hands.

Telling Time Concentration
Teaching Tips and Extensions

- ☆ Photocopy the Telling Time Cards on tagboard. Cut apart the cards, and store sets in separate envelopes before placing them at the center.
- For the Challenge activity, review the rules for "Go Fish."

Materials
- [ ] Telling Time Concentration reproducibles (pages 127–128)
- [ ] small envelopes

Sequence Your Day

1 Draw 3 pictures. Show something you do in the morning, during the day, and at night.

2 Glue your pictures on a piece of paper in the order they happen. Number your pictures 1, 2, and 3.

3 Use your sequence pictures to tell a classmate about your day.

Math Journal Write about or draw times you might need to use a clock on your journal page.

Time

Math Journal

Write about or draw times you might need to use a clock.

Setting a Clock

1 Color and cut out the clock face and hands.

2 Use a brass fastener to put the clock together.

3 Pick 1 time card and say the time out loud.

4 Turn the hands on your clock to match the time. Repeat until all the cards are gone.

 **Challenge** Play with a partner. One person says a sentence that tells a time. *(I went to bed at 8 o'clock.)* The other person sets the clock to match the time.

Instant! Math Centers • K–1 © 2000 Creative Teaching Press

Time

Clock

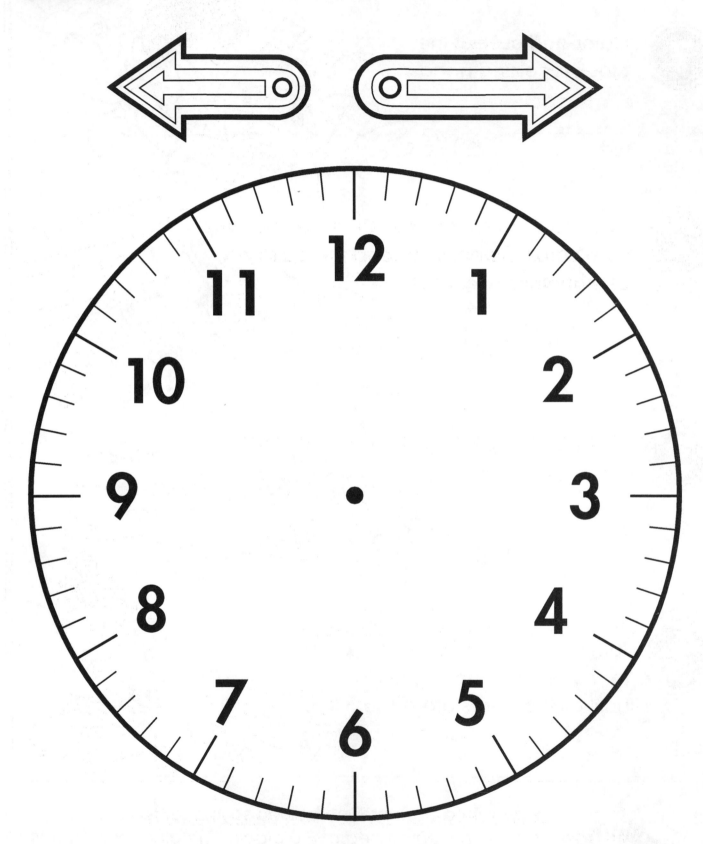

Telling Time Concentration

1 Play with a partner. Spread out all the cards facedown.

2 Turn over 2 cards and say the times out loud. If the cards match, you keep the pair and take another turn.

5 o'clock! They match.

3 If the cards do not match, put them back. It is your partner's turn.

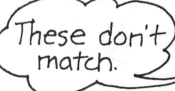

These don't match.

4 Play until all cards are matched up.

Challenge Play a game of "Go Fish" with the same cards.

Time

Telling Time Cards

Instant Math Centers • K–1 © 2000 Creative Teaching Press